PILLARS
OF SUCCESS

Published by CelebrityPress®, Orlando, FL.

CelebrityPress® is a registered trademark.

Printed in the United States of America.

ISBN: 978-1-7334176-4-8
LCCN: 2020904570

Most CelebrityPress® titles are available at special quantity discounts for bulk purchases for sales promotions, premiums, fundraising, and educational use. Special versions or book excerpts can also be created to fit specific needs.

For more information, please write:
CelebrityPress®
520 N. Orlando Ave, #2
Winter Park, FL 32789
or call 1.877.261.4930

Visit us online at: www.CelebrityPressPublishing.com

PILLARS
OF SUCCESS

CelebrityPress®
Winter Park, Florida

CONTENTS

CHAPTER 1

THE TIME-TESTED PILLARS OF SUCCESS

BY JACK CANFIELD

What does it take to achieve the success we want in our lives? In 850 B.C., the Greek philosopher Aristotle documented his "pillars"—or principles—for pursuing success in countless fields of endeavor from metaphysics and biology, to philosophy, medicine, ethics, even politics. Back then, he famously wrote that:

"Quality is not an act, it is a habit."

So what can we learn about the habits that lead to modern-day success? What are the "pillars" we can use to accomplish anything we want in our lives?

DECIDE WHAT SUCCESS LOOKS LIKE TO YOU

For the past 40 years, I've written about, researched, and taught—to millions around the globe—the actions and insights that turn everyday people into high achievers. Not only do these achievers have a highly intentional mindset, but they also incorporate into their lives a set of habits and behaviors that are the hallmark of top-performing people.

What's the first of these behaviors?

These high achievers know what they want out of life. They've already taken the time to decide very specifically what their income, relationships, finances, lifestyle, accomplishments, personal growth and other attributes will be.

If you aspire to join this elite group of purposeful individuals, there's a process I teach for deciding what you want—and for focusing on bringing good things into your life. It's called *The Vision Exercise.*

Begin by listening to some relaxing music and sitting quietly in a comfortable environment. You can either audio-record the following instructions yourself, then play them back during the exercise—or you can have a friend read the instructions to you. Be prepared afterwards to write down your answers in a journal for future use.

Then, begin visualizing your ideal life *exactly the way you want it to be as if you were living it right now.*

1. First, visualize your financial situation. How much money do you have in your savings, how much do you make in income? What is your net worth? How is your cash flow? Next...What does your home look like? Where is it? What color are the walls? Are there paintings hanging in the rooms? What do they look like? Walk through your entire perfect house visually, using your mind's eye.

At this point, don't worry about how you'll get that house. Don't sabotage yourself by saying, "I can't live in Malibu because I don't make enough money." Once you give your mind's eye the picture, your mind will later solve the "not enough money" challenge.

Simply be honest with yourself about what you truly want. Continue visualizing your perfect home. Next, visualize what kind of car you are driving. And then visualize any other possessions you'd like to have.

2. Next, visualize your career. What are you doing in your career? Where are you working? Who are you working with? What kind of clients do you have? What is your compensation like? Is it your own business?

3. Then, focus on your free time, your recreation time. What are you doing with your family and friends in the free time you've created for yourself? What hobbies are you pursuing? What kinds of vacations do you take?

4. Next, visualize your body and your physical health, your emotional and spiritual life. Are you free and open, relaxed, perseverant, in an ecstatic state of bliss all day long? What does that look and feel like?

5. Then move on to visualizing your ideal relationships with your family and friends. What is your relationship with your family like? Who are your friends? What are the quality of your relationships with friends? What do those friendships feel like? Are they loving, supportive, empowering? Could they be better? How do you spend your time together?

6. What about your own personal growth? Do you see yourself going back to school, taking trainings, seeking therapy, counseling or coaching for a past hurt or growing more spiritually?

7. Move on to the geographic community you live in or the community of people you've chosen to interact with. What makes it ideal? What does it look like? What kinds of community activities take place? What about your charitable work? What do you do to help others and make a difference? How often every week do you participate in these activities? Who are you helping?

To help you focus on bringing about this vision for your life, review your notes daily. I also recommend that you write an *affirmation statement** for your most important "wants." Affirmations are vividly detailed statements of you living, working, and enjoying life as if your goals had already been achieved. When you write each of them on a 3x5 notecard or list them in your cell phone, and read them several times a day, affirmations help your mind focus on bringing about your heartfelt desires. Start each statement with the words I am, and write them in the present tense, like this: I am joyfully and gratefully depositing $10,000 a month in my bank account. Then, when you review them throughout the day, visualize what you will be doing once the vision is achieved. What emotions do you feel? What are the sights you see and the sounds you hear? Is anyone else there congratulating you or enjoying the intended outcome with you?

SET GOALS THAT ARE SPECIFIC AND MEASURABLE

Once you know what you want, it's time to turn those "wants" into specific and measurable goals you can focus on every day until you've achieved them. As I often teach my workshop audiences, *A dream without a goal is merely a good idea.* First, set a final results goal such as *I will earn $250,000 by December 31, 2021 at 5 pm.* Then set daily goals for yourself—those "baby steps" you must accomplish on the way to achieving the lifestyle you want?

* To read more about creating and using affirmations to help your brain focus on getting what you want, check out of my book, *Success Affirmations*, at www.jackcanfield.com/store/success-affirmations/

In 1981, George Doran, writing for *Management Review* magazine, introduced the world to the S.M.A.R.T. formula for writing goals and objectives. When you write goals that include the following details, you create goals for your life that are inspiring, focus-worthy, and achievable.

Specific—Each goal should include actual amounts, totals, sizes, or other well-defined terms you want to achieve. By adding specific terms that convey *how much*, your goal becomes clear, understandable and memorable to you (and others). Here are some examples of specific goals: *Walk two miles a day … Call nine sales leads per week … Write 10,000 words a month for my book.*

Measurable—By specifically stating how much in your written goal, you can measure how close you are to accomplishing it. Robin Sharma, author of *The Greatness Guide: Powerful Secrets for Getting to World Class*, tells us that, "What gets measured gets improved." By making your goals measurable, it's easier to keep score, stay on track and strive for bigger gains. Writing down measurable numbers or other specifics also helps you determine when you've achieved your goal.

Accountable—Here's the best part of writing a goal that is specific and measurable: you can be held accountable to it. I recommend that you find an accountability partner—someone who supports you and who will keep you accountable to the goals you've set for your life, including being tough with you if you drift from the goals and dreams you've set for your life. Check in with them at least once a week to report the action you've taken and the progress you've made toward achieving your goal.

Realistic—Many of the goals we have for our lives feel huge and overwhelming. But when you break down your audacious goals into "baby steps," they become achievable with the resources, knowledge, time, and money you have available now—*or that you could acquire.* Don't stop pursuing your goals because you've made them too difficult or outside the realm of your current knowledge. If you don't have the money, time, connections or other resources, make acquiring that knowledge or those connections a "baby step" goal on your away to the ultimate achievement you want?

Time-Based—I teach my students that the most important characteristic of a goal is that it includes a date and time by which you'll achieve the objective. *By December 31, 2025*, you might write, *I will have completely paid off my $268,000 home mortgage.* But before setting a date and time, do your homework—research the process in order to realistically determine a realistic time frame.

TAKE ACTION TOWARD ACHIEVING YOUR GOALS

In the world today, most people are rewarded for action, not for ideas. Yet it's surprising how many people get caught up in planning, deciding, investigating and other preliminary activity—when what they should really be doing is simply taking action on their goals. When you take action, the Universe rewards that action with additional help that can speed you on your way. You also gain feedback about your chosen path or methods.

> *The World Doesn't Pay You for What You Know.*
> *It Pays You for What You Do.*

Many people have had good ideas—some of which led to entirely new industries or never-before-seen ways of making money. The Internet in its infancy was a place where many people had good ideas. But how many of those people took action and created the Google's, Yahoo's, Amazon's and other businesses we know today?

The fact is that, while most people know a lot about making money or getting results or creating advancement in the world, only a few actually get to *enjoy the rewards* of this knowledge (whether

16

financial, professional or congratulatory) simply because they are the select few who take action.

Successful people have a bias for action. More than any other characteristic, action is what separates the successful from the unsuccessful ... the people who actually reap the rewards from those who would merely like to.

Perhaps you, too, had a great idea at one time—only to see it turned into a successful business or a new invention or a popular product by someone else because they took action and you did not.

The reality is that, in the world today, the people who are rewarded are those who take action. We are paid for what we do.

Practice The Rule of 5

When *Chicken Soup for the Soul*® was first published, everyone on the team wanted it to become a New York Times #1 Bestseller. With that goal in mind, we interviewed dozens of book-marketing experts and sought the advice of numerous bestselling authors. We even read a book called *1001 Ways to Market Your Book*. And with literally thousands of strategies we could pursue, to be honest, pursuing our goal became a little overwhelming.

Then one day, we were talking to a friend who reminded us that even the largest tree could be felled simply by swinging an ax at its trunk just five times a day. "Eventually," he concluded, "the tree will have to come down, no matter how large it is."

Out of that advice, we developed The Rule of 5: be committed to accomplishing five simple things every day that will move you closer to completing your goal.

In the case of *Chicken Soup for the Soul*, it meant doing five radio interviews a day. Or sending out five review copies to newspapers every day. Or asking five pastors to use a story from the book in their sermons. Or calling five companies to encourage them to buy a copy for all their employees. Or sending out five press releases a day. And on and on ... every day for more than two years. Not only was it worth it, but in two years the book went on to reach #1 on the *New York Times* and *USA Today* bestseller lists—and has also sold more than 11 million copies in the United States and many millions more in nearly 50 languages worldwide.

What could you do in your life if you created an inspiring goal, then did five things every day to bring you closer to achieving it?

When Obstacles Appear, Make Sure You Know Which Kind They Are

As you take action, many of your most important goals will require you to learn new skills, meet new people and apply yourself to a number of difficult tasks. Additionally, you'll have to overcome some very daunting obstacles starting at almost the moment you set a new goal. I call these obstacles *considerations, fears* and *roadblocks*.

Unfortunately, even the slightest obstacle stops most people from going any further, which is a shame since most can be easily overcome and usually aren't stopping points at all. Let's take a look:

Considerations—When you decide to pursue an important new goal such as starting a business or growing your income or doubling your time-off, suddenly thoughts enter your head such as *My family will suffer if I'm focused on making money or I'll have to convince my wife this will work, or I can't afford to take 6 weeks away from my business.* Far from an actual impediment, *considerations* are merely thoughts in your head telling you all the reasons why your goal is impossible or something you shouldn't pursue. Sometimes they're our low self-esteem talking to us. Other times, they are issues that have not surfaced before—which lets us deal with them at last and move on.

Fears—Fears, on the other hand, are simply feelings that aren't usually based upon actual circumstances. For instance, in recruiting investors for a new business you want to start, you might fear being rejected or being told that your dream business is a bad idea. But can this rejection or feedback alone stop you (or anyone) from building a thriving new business Of course not. While you might fear looking foolish or awkward in the beginning, the *fear itself* is not really a stopping point. Feel the fear and take action anyway.

Roadblocks—Finally, you may encounter *roadblocks*. These are conditions that are beyond your control such as a government regulation that prohibits what you want to do or a physical ailment that limits you or having a lack of money to start your business. While roadblocks might give you pause, more often they simply require you to work out an alternate approach that—in the process of developing it—you might actually create a better or faster way of reaching your goal. Be aware that roadblocks are situations that just exist in the world. They aren't directed specifically at you nor are they another example of, "Gee, the world hates me." Deal with them and move on.

Considerations, fears and roadblocks will always come up, particularly when you've set a truly monumental goal for yourself. Your job is to recognize them for what they are … and aren't. They aren't stopping points or reasons for you not to pursue your goal. They are validation that your goal is worthwhile. They are opportunities for you to grow as a person—practicing new skills, galvanizing beliefs and gaining self-assurance. And they are the means to face your fears, and overcome the thoughts, emotions and feelings that have likely been holding you back in other areas of your life.

RESPOND DIFFERENTLY TO LIFE'S CURVEBALLS

Another phenomenon that will occur as you begin taking focused action toward achieving your goals is that you'll begin to think, act, and "show up" differently. Little by little, you'll gain more experience, better knowledge, extra confidence, and greater self-esteem. Perhaps the most important outcome of pursuing your goals is *who you will become as a person* by simply going after your dreams. You'll be much better prepared to respond with assurance when life throws you curveballs—an unexpected crisis or a unique opportunity, for instance. You'll be better prepared to create a better outcome for yourself and your future.

In reality, our responses to life's events are all that stand between us experiencing a negative outcome or a positive one. To help you remember how important your responses are, there's a formula I teach: E+R=O.

Event + Response = Outcome

Every result or **outcome (O)** we get in life is a direct result of our **response (R)** to the countless **events (E)** that occur every day. In other words, whether our outcomes are financial success or financial scarcity, helpful relationships or disconnection, easy workdays or repeated frustration—all depends on how we respond to the events that occur in our lives.

Of course, how you respond is always your choice. You can choose to either blame the event—or you can take 100% responsibility for your response to it. Let's take a look:

1. **You can blame the event (E) for results you don't like (O).** What are some examples of events that can show up in anyone's life? A bad economy, workplace politics, an inattentive spouse, government or industry regulations, the city you live in, your level of education, competition on the Internet, the fact that you have small children or aging

parents to care for, and on and on. Many situations can't be helped; they just are. But if these situations were the deciding factor in whether someone was successful or not— no one would ever achieve anything.

Henry Ford would never have built the automobile, Margaret Thatcher would never have been elected Prime Minister of England, and Marc Andreessen would never have developed a way to browse the Internet. For every event that stops millions of people from getting what they want, hundreds of other people face that same event and succeed.

2. **You can decide instead to respond (R) differently the next time and automatically change the outcome (O) you get**. With this single decision, suddenly you'll begin to act with purpose. When faced with any event, you'll think consciously about your desired outcomes—then control your actions, behaviors and thoughts so they move you toward success instead of keeping you in victimhood.

After all, the only thing you really *can* change is your response to events—that is, how you accomplish your goals in spite of obvious roadblocks, lack of support, negative people in your life, and so on.

If you want a better experience, you need only change your responses to the events that occur in your life. Change your thoughts of lack or helplessness into thoughts of abundance and action. Change the way you "see" yourself in your mind's eye to positive pictures of your exciting future with your own successful business. Change your non-productive activity into focused, consistent effort and productive work habits.

Taking 100% Responsibility for How
You Respond Gives You More Power

When you step into this position of power by consciously

choosing how you'll respond, it becomes immediately clear that you either actively create things in your life or you *allow them to happen* through sheer inaction—including creating or allowing things you may not like.

For example, let's say you start a small business. As the business grows rapidly, you decide to hire an outside bookkeeper. Confident you've found the right person, you give her access to the online bill paying system. Soon, weekly reports show up less and less frequently. Instead of questioning her, you blithely assume she knows what she's doing. One day, your banker calls. Though your business had been earning over $50,000 a month, your account is now overdrawn, and several substantial checks are being presented for payment. When you telephone the bookkeeper, your calls are not returned. A visit to the bank reveals tens of thousands of dollars' worth of checks written to sham companies and people you don't know. You have to face that you created this situation. You gave total authority over your finances to someone you thought was "smarter" than you.

In other situations, you *allow* things to *happen to you* through inaction. You're unwilling to do the uncomfortable, say what is necessary, take actions others may not like, or make demands.

- You didn't attend company sales trainings because you were too busy, and now you're being passed over for a promotion to someone younger with fewer years at the company.
- You ignored your intuition and let the kids bring home a dog from the local pet rescue. Now your family's schedule is tied to his care, there's pet hair everywhere, and his constant barking is intolerable.
- You spent your paychecks instead of setting aside a portion for savings, and now a sudden family emergency has become a full-blown financial crisis.

Realize that you are not the victim here. In every situation, you passively allowed these outcomes to happen through inaction.

You didn't improve your skills, save your money, say no, or dedicate the time necessary to change the outcome.

The E+R=O formula is a powerful reminder that keeps us focused on our goals.

* * * *

In conclusion, these pillars of success are the hallmarks of focused, goal-oriented, peak-performing people. In fact, setting goals daily, taking specific action, and responding differently to life's events is simply what top achievers do.

It's what you, too, can practice in your life in order to excel in any area you desire. First decide what you want, then let these success principles carry you forward to achieve the life you dream of … and deserve.

About Jack

Known as America's #1 Success Coach, Jack Canfield is the CEO of the Canfield Training Group in Santa Barbara, CA, which trains and coaches entrepreneurs, corporate leaders, managers, sales professionals and the general public in how to accelerate the achievement of their personal, professional and financial goals.

Jack Canfield is best known as the coauthor of the #1 *New York Times* bestselling *Chicken Soup for the Soul®* book series, which has sold more than 500 million books in 47 languages, including 11 *New York Times* #1 bestsellers. As the CEO of Chicken Soup for the Soul Enterprises he helped grow the *Chicken Soup for the Soul®* brand into a virtual empire of books, children's books, audios, videos, CDs, classroom materials, a syndicated column and a television show, as well as a vigorous program of licensed products that includes everything from clothing and board games to nutraceuticals and a successful line of *Chicken Soup for the Pet Lover's Soul®* cat and dog foods.

His other books include *The Success Principles™: How to Get from Where You Are to Where You Want to Be* (recently revised as the 10th Anniversary Edition), *The Success Principles for Teens, The Aladdin Factor, Dare to Win, Heart at Work, The Power of Focus: How to Hit Your Personal, Financial and Business Goals with Absolute Certainty, You've Got to Read This Book, Tapping into Ultimate Success, Jack Canfield's Key to Living the Law of Attraction,* his recent novel, T*he Golden Motorcycle Gang: A Story of Transformation* and *The 30-Day Sobriety Solution.*

Jack is a dynamic speaker and was recently inducted into the National Speakers Association's Speakers Hall of Fame. He has appeared on more than 1000 radio and television shows including Oprah, Montel, Larry King Live, The Today Show, Fox and Friends, and 2 hour-long PBS Specials devoted exclusively to his work. Jack is also a featured teacher in 12 movies including *The Secret, The Meta-Secret, The Truth, The Keeper of the Keys, Tapping into the Source,* and *The Tapping Solution.* Jack was also honored recently with a documentary that was produced about his life and teachings, *The Soul of Success: The Jack Canfield Story.*

Jack has personally helped hundreds of thousands of people on six different continents become multi-millionaires, business leaders, best-selling authors, leading sales professionals, successful entrepreneurs, and world-class athletes while at the same time creating balanced, fulfilling and healthy lives.

His corporate clients have included Virgin Records, SONY Pictures, Daimler-Chrysler, Federal Express, GE, Johnson & Johnson, Merrill Lynch, Campbell's Soup, Re/Max, The Million Dollar Forum, The Million Dollar Roundtable, The Young Entrepreneurs Organization, The Young Presidents Organization, the Executive Committee, and the World Business Council.

Jack is the founder of the Transformational Leadership Council and a member of Evolutionary Leaders, two groups devoted to helping create a world that works for everyone.

Jack is a graduate of Harvard, earned his M.Ed. from the University of Massachusetts, and has received three honorary doctorates in psychology and public service. He is married, has three children, two step-children and a grandson.

For more information, visit:
- www.JackCanfield.com
- www.CanfieldTraintheTrainer.com

CHAPTER 2

MISSION CRITICAL: ENGAGING AND EMPOWERING SUPER-WOMEN IN TECHNOLOGY
FOUR STEPS FOR SUCCESS IN TECH

BY NICOLE SCHEFFLER

We're at a unique point in history where the things we are building are going to significantly impact our social, political, economic, and personal lives.
~ Anita Borg, Celebrated computer scientist &
Women-in-Technology advocate

According to 2018 research, most Americans – nearly 80% – consider gender diversity in the workplace important.[1] While by and large the U.S. population still champions the country's founding principles of equality and opportunity, in 2019 only 25% of women held computing jobs. Additionally, just 12% of engineers at lucrative, high-potential Silicon Valley startups were women.[2] When it comes to the technology field, we still have work to do to achieve gender equality. Increasing the number of

1 https://www.catalyst.org/research/why-diversity-and-inclusion-matter/
2 https://www.dreamhost.com/blog/state-of-women-in-tech/

women is just one essential facet of true diversity and is the focus of this chapter.

As a woman with more than 15 years' tenure in the industry, I've seen firsthand how gender parity in technology can amplify creativity and innovation. Beyond the altruistic case for equality, it is important to understand the proven business and societal benefits from increasing ratios of women in technology. Studies show workforce diversity boosts innovation, profitability, and progress. It's clear that the global environmental outlook, among other worldwide issues, is of increasing concern to both prominent scientists worldwide and respected organizations, like the United Nations. We need solutions to big problems as quickly as possible. This alone justifies aggressive investments in diversity, equity, and inclusion.

Empowering women in technology, and those considering a tech career path, with tools to guide their own success, is important. However, companies must understand the benefits of investing in formal diversity and inclusion programs that support this movement. It needs to be more than checking a box. We must intrinsically interweave these efforts into our education system and company cultures, so that women feel the impact. This combination of corporate investment and personal commitment to success will help attract and retain women in technology. Then, we will have more technically savvy women who become Super Heroes that develop world-saving technologies.

NURTURING GENDER EQUALITY DRAWS TOP TALENT

There is substantial proof that increasing women's representation in technology is good for business and contributes to a flourishing culture. "When a company's culture feels fair and inclusive, women and underrepresented groups are happier and likely to thrive,"[3] research by the global Catalyst nonprofit finds. The

3 https://www.catalyst.org/research/why-diversity-and-inclusion-matter/

organization, dedicated to advancing women in the workplace, adds, "The more psychologically safe employees feel at work, the more likely they are to feel included in work groups." Open company cultures foster positive, inclusive workplaces – the kind that retain talented women.[4]

The best companies are often recognized and rewarded for their efforts. This helps them attract top talent to drive innovation and propel success. For example, in 2019 the prestigious technology nonprofit AnitaB.org awarded multinational Bank of America its 2019 Top Company for Women Technologists, recognizing the financial giant's inclusive culture inside and outside the workplace.[5] Great Place to Work just recognized the vast corporate social responsibility and diversity efforts of global tech firm Cisco by naming them #1 World's Best Workplace in 2019.[6] Even with this progress, there is still much work to be done.

Clearly, culture matters. Companies with well-defined diversity and inclusion cultures create productive environments. Such atmospheres encourage people to give their best at the workplace, ultimately increasing significant contributions and reducing talent turnover.

TEAM DIVERSITY BOOSTS PRODUCTIVITY, PROFITABILITY

Overwhelming statistics point to the success of diverse teams, including increased productivity, and creativity. Greater gender balance among corporate leadership yields higher stock values and profitability.[7] A study spanning 22,000 globally-traded public companies across 91 countries shows having 30% women in

---

4 ibid., p.28

5 https://anitab.org/profiles/top-companies/bank-america-women-technologists/

6 https://www.greatplacetowork.com/best-workplaces-international/world-s-best-workplaces/2019

7 https://www.piie.com/publications/working-papers/gender-diversity-profitable-evidence-global-survey

leadership created a 6% greater net profit margin.[8] Additionally, economic researchers from McKinsey Global Institute estimated in 2015 that workplace gender parity could increase global output by more than 25%.[9] Parity can also cut costs, since gender-diverse boards are associated with more effective risk management practices when investing in research and development.[10] *It literally pays to have more women represented across all organizational levels.*

Diversity also unlocks innovation and drives market growth.[11] Teams comprising different viewpoints or thinking styles solve problems faster and originate innovation. The earlier referenced Catalyst study also shows companies with "diversity in management earned 38% more revenue, on average, from innovative products and services in the last three years," than companies lacking diversity. Diverse teams also drive deeper customer engagement. Teams are 158% more likely to understand the customer when they have at least one trait in common with their customer's gender, race, age, sex, or culture.[12]

GLOBAL CHALLENGES DEMAND MULTIFACETED APPROACHES

Women are key to inclusive, profitable cultures, and, as the world changes, the urgency to bring more of us to the table increases. Civilization's future will provide no shortage of challenges, from uncontrollable wildfires to rising sea levels.[13] There are few future hurdles that we can't overcome with the right solution. Whether it's leveraging the Internet of Things (IoT) to save endangered

8   https://qz.com/612086/huge-study-find-that-companies-with-more-women-leaders-are-more-profitable/

9   https://www.mckinsey.com/featured-insights/gender-equality/women-in-the-workplace-2019

10 https://www.catalyst.org/research/why-diversity-and-inclusion-matter/

11 https://hbr.org/2013/12/how-diversity-can-drive-innovation

12 https://www.catalyst.org/research/why-diversity-and-inclusion-matter/

13 https://www.bbc.com/future/article/20170713-what-will-the-challenges-of-2050-be

species or deploying connected roadways to keep drivers safer in inclement weather, technology is critical to addressing future challenges. As they have throughout history, contributions from skilled, creative women technologists drive future advances.

Now that we have made the data-driven case for collective investment in diversity for companies, let's explore how women technologists can accelerate their own journeys as individuals. We can all do our part to influence positive change in our workplace, but that requires investment and participation at all levels of many organizations over time. Another way to empower women in technology is to guide their own personal development. This starts within the individual and can be done immediately, while we work together to create this wholistic, diverse culture in more companies.

CHAMPIONING SUCCESS AND CREATING SUPERHEROES

Although I work as an engineer in the corporate world by day, I wear my superhero cape nights and weekends to serve the community with my own technical talents. I have met women and men from so many different walks of life – each with their own gifts and stories – who have expanded my knowledge and horizons.

My own career growth stems from following key best practices inspired through community engagement, encounters with technology leaders, Jack Canfield's *Success Principles*[14], and women-in-tech conferences. As a result, I adopted these guiding success principles in a simple, four-step "superheroine" framework. Sharing these is how I want to give back to the next generation of Super Women in tech.

---

14 http://www.thesuccessprinciples.com/

FOUR STEPS FOR SUCCESS IN TECH[15]

1. Take full responsibility while embracing feedback

Owning our experience is 100% our responsibility. Motivational speaker Zig Ziglar said, "Your attitude, not your aptitude, will determine your altitude." As a minority in tech, it can be easy in the face of statistics to blame others for tough situations. However, I believe we are each responsible for consciously creating our own positive career paths. Challenges that arise throughout our careers are accompanied by numerous opportunities to respond. Our response inevitably shapes outcomes. We must own the challenges. When we pause, think, and thoughtfully react, or choose not to react, we take charge of the situation, helping shape it and ourselves. This empowers educated, intentional career choices and outcomes.

Taking responsibility paired with requesting, and accepting, feedback spurs growth. Feedback can guide us and help diversify our views. Soliciting feedback shows commitment to achieving goals. Considering feedback can expand horizons and inform solutions. Examining wide feedback allows us to choose relevant options, and store other vantage points for future reference, if not immediately applicable.

In my personal life, as someone relatively new to motherhood, I've discovered people freely offer advice on everything – from labor to how to raise a child. While I can't (and don't) follow every suggestion, I do incorporate feedback that resonates with my values and goals. The same is true for career advice. The more feedback we accrue, the more enlightened our view, and the more useful for considerations when taking the next step.

2. Set goals and act

Success in technology can be achieved by aligning career

---

15 https://www.catalyst.org/research/why-diversity-and-inclusion-matter/

goals with work we enjoy. Goals are as important to our careers as they are to every other area of our lives – finances, relationships, health, and spiritual arenas included. Set SMART goals (Specific, Measurable, Attainable, Relevant, and Time-bound) in writing. Share them with others, and continually revisit and revise them.

Once we set goals aligned to our strengths and passions, we must act to achieve them. Some of us struggle to take the first step. Behind our waiting for the perfect time, or opportunity, is often an unconscious, intrinsic fear of failure. Action is what separates success from failure. Remember that real achievement is never about perfection, it is always about progress. To realize our dreams, we must put ideas into motion, learn from experiences, and keep evolving.

Setting goals and acting are inextricably connected. We can set goals all day, but if we don't act, we spend our lives dreaming of the possibilities. When we work toward the lives we desire and follow career paths we enjoy, every step forward is progress. My personal route has taken me from database creation and management, to coding, networking, technical marketing, and leadership, based on what I enjoy and where my strengths are of utmost value to the business. My growth stems from a clear combination of goals, action, and no fear of failure.

3. Visualize the achievements you desire

Harnessing the power of visualization can help us advance toward our established goals. Taking time to imagine or act as if we have achieved our goals has substantial benefits. It can activate the subconscious mind, engaging new parts of the brain to access resources we haven't previously leveraged. This can open our eyes to see people and opportunities that move us toward our envisioned futures.

While visualization helps us embrace positive opportunities, it can also help us tackle and overcome challenges, or push us to look at things in a different light. For example, when I find myself the only woman in the room, I choose to discover and focus on where I can have a positive impact, and how I can support the team. I have already visualized my career success, so my contributions every day on the team are a pathway to that destination. That can't happen if I divert my attention to things that are not part of my goals or envisioned future.

4. Find your tribe and give back

The last, and perhaps most important component for women forging a path in technology is finding and building community. Community embodies people who positively impact our journeys. For me it is a diverse group of women and men, many of whom have been my mentors. You may already have a personal and/or professional tribe. Embracing a positive, goal-oriented mindset requires people who uplift and inspire us and provide critical, supportive feedback that helps us learn and grow. Choose your tribe wisely and constantly evaluate for adjustments.

I call this group my "personal board of directors" because they are each unique. Some are even my mentees, but all have strengths I can call on for a mentor "moment" in any situation. Mentoring does not always occur as an in-depth 1:1, consistent interaction. So, this board model allows me to access the right perspective at the right time, depending on the situation.

Local "women in technology" groups are ripe with networking and growth opportunities. Seek groups who share a passion for empowering women in technology, who convene specialists in your technical area, or who allow you to contribute skills towards causes about which you're passionate. These groups offer rich learning and leadership opportunities outside the corporate structure, while providing a safe place to fail. Finding our tribes and giving back helps us think bigger, expanding our worlds.

Those are just a few things you can do for your own success as a women in tech, and we are all responsible for supporting and engaging in corporate diversity programs. As women in technology, we are changing the world by:

- producing innovative solutions to global challenges
- engaging in diverse customer interactions
- building stronger company cultures
- contributing to higher corporate earnings

These benefits should offer intrinsic motivation for organizations to invest in diversity and inclusion. We need women in tech now, more than ever, to invent and lead the development of solutions to make our world a more sustainable, safe place. Let's get our capes ready because the world needs us and we are ready for success.

About Nicole

Nicole Scheffler is a modern *digital renaissance woman* – a "Digissance Woman," with robust technology skills, broad business background, and a passion for empowering women to succeed in tech.

Nicole began in the startup space as a programmer, moved to business analyst for Fidelity Investments, and has grown her career significantly at tech giant Cisco Systems. Crain's Detroit Business honored her among its 2018 Notable Women in Tech, and Cisco awarded her its esteemed Chairman's Club, a distinction given to less than 1% of its worldwide sales force. Her Cisco career spans tenures as a systems engineer, technical marketing engineer, and security consulting engineer. Most recently, she migrated to Cisco's Channel Operations. There, she leads strategy for the Americas Partner Engineering Organization, throughout North and Latin America, while managing a highly-experienced technical engineering team.

Nicole co-founded the award-winning "Diva Tech Talk" podcast – a collection of women sharing their motivational career journeys in technology to inspire other women to pursue and expand their own careers in the space. As the first women in tech-focused podcast to market, "Diva Tech Talk" has won significant honors since its 2015 launch, including five prized Association of Women in Communication Clarion Awards. Most recently, it received a 2019 The People's Choice Podcast Award nomination. Nicole also covered women in technology as a MITechNews.com Associate Editor.

Nicole's formal education includes a bachelor's degree in Business Computer Information Systems and a master's degree in Information Technology from the University of North Texas, where she was chosen to speak at graduation. Her work as an adjunct professor began at the age of 26 – covering the Information Warfare/Security, Wireless Security, Biometrics Fundamentals, and VoIP Fundamentals arenas. She's also taught through Cisco's skill-building Networking Academy, offering Cisco Certification courses, and she's earned multiple industry certifications, including the Cisco Certified Networking Associate up to the Cisco Certified Internetwork Expert written.

Motivating and empowering others is in Nicole's DNA. Every day, she works to positively impact communities worldwide. She leads and volunteers generously for organizations that include Michigan Council of Women in Technology Foundation and Women of Cisco. She's also founded both a nonprofit and a technology user group. As a longtime advocate for STEM Women, she embraces the idea that, "One person can't do everything, but everyone can do something." Nicole also volunteers for many local organizations, often leveraging her social media skills.

She also has a track record of sharing her passion through speaking engagements. To date, she has delivered nine keynote addresses and over 30 general talks and panels. Her areas of expertise include Women's Empowerment, Networking, Security, IoT, Leadership, Programming, and Gratitude.

Nicole lives her principles of leadership, community, giving, and teaching, daily – and works to inspire others to follow suit. In 2020, she will complete her Canfield Success Principles Trainer Certification, create courses to share these with other women in tech, and publish a kids' book to encourage girls in STEM. She lives in Michigan with her husband and daughter.

Nicole would love to connect:
- www.digissancewoman.com
- https://twitter.com/tech_NICOLE
- https://www.linkedin.com/in/nicole/

CHAPTER 3

WHAT A DIFFERENCE A DAY CAN MAKE IN YOUR LIFE

BY PAT ZIEMER

You just can't beat a person who never gives up.
~ Babe Ruth

I share this information with you to show the background and life circumstances we were experiencing when our Magna Wave PEMF (Pulsed Electro-Magnetic Fields) journey began. While everyone's story and reasoning when starting a business are different, what is the same is that it takes belief, dedication, and perseverance to achieve the success you desire.

In 2001, I was in the aviation industry, selling air charter services and corporate jet aircraft. The terrorist attacks of 9/11 devastated the aviation industry and put me out of business. I needed something to do and a friend who knew that I had been around horses all of my life, asked me if I would represent his PEMF therapy products at Churchill Downs in Kentucky and area horse shows.

In June of 2002, I began my PEMF journey by providing low

power PEMF equipment to the equine industry. I worked selling the low-powered PEMF equipment and traveled extensively throughout the United States and Canada selling and training others in the use of PEMF equipment. I was first exposed to high-powered PEMF devices in 2005. I was not sold on the equipment because I did not feel that it was comfortable for the client or easy to use in the equine world. Business was good with my company, so I stayed the course with my current supplier.

In early 2006, we lost our oldest son from surgical complications associated with an unknown genetic heart condition. My life took a spiral and became psychologically and financially challenging for more than a year. In the summer of 2007, while working on getting off of antidepressants and on getting my work-life back together, my wife Debi and I were introduced to the high-powered PEMF device that would change our experience and the direction of my career.

Debi was a school teacher, and she had taken a fall on ice while walking her students between buildings in 2005. As a result, she had severe compression of her upper spine, and she had three herniated discs. She experienced continual pain and limited mobility of her left arm and shoulder. I used all of the devices available to us, including low-power PEMF and laser therapy, to try to help her situation. While she got some relief, she did not experience any reversal of the case. A horse trainer friend of mine at Santa Anita race track in California called me and told me about this machine they were using on their horses and how well it was working. He got me the name of the manufacturer and suggested that I call to get more information.

That same day, while at a horse show in Atlanta, a customer came up to me and told me about a similar device from another manufacturer, and she also gave me a name and a number. I felt that someone was trying to tell me something, so I called them both. It turns out that both were going to be at an anti-aging conference in Orlando, Florida. We decided to go and find out first-hand about this high-powered PEMF product. While attending a machine demonstration session at the show, they asked for a volunteer from the audience to try the machine. Debi looked at me and said that she would do it because nothing had worked for her and that this new machine probably would not work either, then we could leave and go back to Ocala. She volunteered, went to the stage, sat in a chair, and had her shoulder treated for eight minutes. When she stood up and went to move her arm as directed, she had complete mobility and no pain in her back or shoulder. With tears in her eyes as she looked at me, and I immediately knew that we were going to have to find a way to get a machine.

I spent the next day talking with both companies about the opportunities available. One company was brand new and was just beginning the manufacturing process, and the other had been manufacturing for a few years. Remember, I was psychologically and financially down, but I knew that Debi wanted a machine.

I needed to find a way to make the situation work. Neither company was deep into the horse world, and there were only a few machines in use in the industry. I told both companies about my equine background with PEMF and about my spending the last six years working with leading thoroughbred and hunter-jumper trainers around the world. I told them that I would present the machine to the equine world and that I would deliver the equine market.

I also outlined the changes about timers, packaging, and transporting the unit that needed to be changed on the device to make it more acceptable and easier to use in the equine environment. One believed me, and one somewhat did not think that I genuinely had the necessary contacts. The one who believed me asked me to write him a check, that he would hold, and that I could begin to make payments. I accepted the offer, and we were in business and literally off to the races.

We received our machine in October and officially started the day after Thanksgiving of 2007 with a great tool, determination, and $50.00 in my pocket. We paid off the machine in less than a year($21,000.00), and we grew to become, and remain, one of the largest distributors for the manufacturer. A significant element that contributed to our success is that the machine worked. Debi's arm and back no longer bothered her, and both of us came to experience a sense of wellbeing and less depression by using the machine, which allowed us both to get off of antidepressants. The doctors still, to this day, cannot figure out why her arm and back no longer bother her when they look at her x-rays.

CERTIFICATION CASE STUDY

Before starting in 2007, I was already working in the horse industry, selling low power PEMF therapy devices. Still, with this new device, which we branded as Magna Wave, I began to provide the therapy treatments instead of just selling devices. But providing the treatments was an obstacle because I identified around the country as an equipment salesperson and not a therapist. Consequently, some people felt that I did not have the qualifications to be a therapist. I did have a secondary college degree in the areas of physiology, anatomy, and pathology, so my one-on-one customer service challenge became the one-on-one discussions on my education as a basis for my understanding and qualification to provide the therapy.

While that story helped the cause, the real catalyst for the business growth was that the treatment worked. In the beginning, I was the "crazy guy," pulling around this new therapy machine. Then I became "Dr. Voodoo" with this weird machine that did seem to work. Later, I became the guy that veterinarians considered competition, and it must be potentially harmful, or, at best, illegal. Over time the therapy became so popular that the veterinary community, for the most part, embraced it. At this point, most of the customer service discussions were face-to-face or on the phone. We had a necessary web presence, but we did not have the traffic for any measurable contact or customer service through the site.

The growth at this point was as a result of direct sales and contact with my potential customers. The methods worked, but I soon learned that I needed to connect with my customers from all over the country in a timely and efficient manner. Thus I engaged the internet and the burgeoning social media outlets, and that is when things got messy. There was so much to learn, and when I would learn what to do, it would change. I found myself starting again. I was drowning in a pool of technical information and strategies from everyone and their brother dealing with their ideal online marketing recommendations.

I found myself buying a product, starting to learn it, and then a week later, someone had the next best thing, and I would jump in and start again. My wife called it acting like a squirrel, or what many call the shiny object syndrome. In 2011, I once again purchased a new marketing product and embarked on the learning and implementation path. The difference this time was a support community that could answer questions. The community turned into a mastermind where we could all grow and learn from each other, which was incredibly helpful. If you do not participate in a mastermind or coaching community, start tomorrow.

For the first years, my wife and I traveled the country in a motorhome providing treatments. We were starting to do well, and as you might suspect, people began inquiring about purchasing machines to offer the therapy. I did not know where this would go, but I started selling the devices and training the new practitioners. It seemed that wherever we would travel, we would find someone wanting to purchase the equipment and begin working with their customers. The training was not an issue because I was there treating horses that provided the perfect way to train the new machine owners.

Over the next three years, we grew to nearly 100 practitioners around the country, and I had to quit treating so as not to compete with the new practitioners. As you can imagine, the customer service at that point was still pretty much face-to-face and handled entirely by me, as I was still pretty much a one-person show.

By this time, our business revenue had grown to the mid-to-upper six figures, and it seemed to plateau there for three years. I knew that I needed to enhance education, and I wanted to offer training and certification as part of the program. I worked with several different platforms, but I just could not get the system going. The work and time involved seemed insurmountable. I was actively working on the internet and social networks to grow the business because we learned that our primary customers, horsemen, and horsewomen, were active on sites like Facebook.

In 2010, we discovered that almost 90% of our business was in some manner moving through Facebook. Because of this, we were able to sell the RV and return to Louisville and travel less. Customer service was originating and being handled through Facebook, LinkedIn, and our website.

It was late 2011 when I discovered the TPNI Engage marketing system. TPNI Engage provided an email and text auto-responder system and list building tools that I desperately needed for customer service and follow up. I bought into the system to use it to market our products, and our practitioner's services. We now offer these services in-house, custom-tailored for our practitioner network that has grown to nearly twenty-five hundred practitioners. While attending a TPNI event, I was sitting with a group, and I was discussing my need for a certification program, when one member of the group looked at me and said you could build the program within TPNI Engage, just duplicate their program. I was in awe. Could it be that easy?

Within a week of my returning home from the event, the basis of my certification program was in place. All I did was change the wording where necessary to reflect the machine usage. The next thing I had to do was work out the logistics of promotional videos, recording the webinars, editing, hosting, SEO, and a myriad of other details. Ultimately, I sought out the help of my mastermind, for guidance on each step of the way in producing the Magna Wave certification program.

This group suggested what programs to use and, in most cases, helped me avoid learning curves to get quick implementation. The bones were in place in two weeks. The program launched within four weeks and the live webinar classes were completed, recorded, and edited within ten weeks. The certification program has now successfully been running for the past ten years. We have added modules for humans and small animals in addition to the initial equine training. So the question is, how did the program affect the business?

The impact was immediate and dramatic. Over the first 30 to 60 days, sales were up 40%, and the driving force was the certification process. Some racing jurisdictions now require the certification for access to the grounds with our type of device. We became experts in the field, and our credibility and respect increased proportionately. This momentum drove the business to seven figures. This past year, we surpassed eight figures and we are 40% ahead of last year at this time. With sales tripling within two years, customer service became the focal point of our customer interaction.

The staff grew from my wife and me to include our daughter Alane and then Erin joined us as our Director of Certification and Training. We have now grown to over twenty-five full-time staff members. In 2017, I hired an outside marketing company on a dare that for every dollar we put in, they would return two or three dollars in new revenue. I started with a modest but real budget that has increased to a dizzying amount by some standards, but the payback has been right on track. Our marketing has included every platform covered earlier, and our staff provides the multi-source customer service for our increasing customer base.

I continue to meet with my mastermind group weekly, and I seek advice about what I am currently working to accomplish. The answers I receive continue to give me the direction I need and cuts implementation time in half or more. You, too, can benefit from this brain trust of experts in the ever-changing world of internet and offline marketing. If you do not ask for help, you will spend unnecessary time learning, or if you can ask for help, you will save time and ultimately make more money. My accountant used to tell me it is not how fast you find a hole, it's how quickly you fill it. Make expert marketing and superior customer service your priority, and you will not have as many holes to fill.

Health and Wellness utilizing Magna Wave PEMF have become my passion, and I now dedicate my life and time to helping thousands of people to gain financial independence and success in their life that they desire. I thank God every day for the opportunity to do this. I am available to help; just let me know.

About Pat

Pat Ziemer is the owner of Magna Wave PEMF. PEMF is the application of High Voltage Pulsed Electro-Magnetic Fields into the body that reduce inflammation and relieve pain, allowing for the body to better heal itself. Pat has been working full time with PEMF since 2002. The company's therapy devices are used extensively on racehorses, performance horses, and even professional athletes. Seven recent Kentucky Derby winners and numerous world champions in many horse disciplines utilize the therapy regularly.

Many NFL, MLB, NBA, NHL and MLS teams utilize Magna Wave Therapy. In 2007, Pat acquired the rights to the PEMF device, repackaged it, branded it as Magna Wave and hit the road marketing the Magna Wave brand. Since 2007, the company has placed over 2000 Magna Wave devices into the market for private and professional use. Magna Wave now services the human, small animal, and equine markets.

You can find Pat on LinkedIn at: Patrick Ziemer.

CHAPTER 4

generationDREAM

BY PHYLLIS PORTER TURNER

Walt Disney, Eva Manette Porter, Martin Luther King, Jr., Thomas Edison, Oprah Winfrey, Frederick August Otto (FAO) Schwarz, Amelia Earhart, Louis Braille, Babe Ruth, me and YOU! What is the common thread that exists between us and many more throughout our past present and future? We are a generation of DREAMERS making a life-changing difference in the world! We are not defined by time, age, gender, race, nationality, culture, demographics or socioeconomics.

We are generationDREAM!!!

"Have you ever had a dream that seemed to reach beyond the farthest star at night? And have you ever wished upon that star as it shines up in the sky so very bright? Have you ever wondered if your life could make a difference in this world? Well, you're just a dream away....let your imagination soar!" These are some of the lyrics I wrote 17 years ago to the song entitled (yes, you guessed it), "DREAM"! I was at a stage in life where I wanted to make a difference in the world, but I didn't know exactly how that was going to happen or even remotely what that would look like. All I knew is that I had a burning desire down in the depths of by soul to make my little life count in this great big world.

A very shy girl growing up in DeRidder, LA, I was quite challenged in believing in myself. I was so shy that when someone simply looked at me, I thought they had a problem with me and I would usually cry to my mother, "Momma, they're looking at me!" When I was in middle school, I began to emerge from my shell and tossed around the idea of trying out for cheerleader, which was very scary to me. I'll never forget what my mother told me when I ran it by her. She said that I'd have a 100% chance of NOT making it if I didn't try, but a great chance if I did. Well, I decided to take my chances. I tried and somehow made it!! This was the beginning of a lifetime of dreaming, believing and becoming generationDREAM.

THE generationDREAM ROADMAP

— DREAM...
— Dream BEYOND the stars!

We've all heard the saying, 'shoot for the stars' defined as, "To set one's goals or ambitions very high; to try to attain or achieve something particularly difficult." Michelangelo once said that the greatest danger for most of us is not that our aim is too high and we miss it, but that it is too low and we hit it. Instead of "shooting for the stars", I say, "Dream BEYOND the stars!"

Don't have small dreams. Don't aim low and hit. Aim high with your dreams ... BEYOND the stars, so when you miss, you'll actually hit your dream and become the shining star of who you are.

Wildly IMPOSSIBLE, crazy IMPROBABLE dreams are the best dreams to have; and most often, these ideas come from the simple life that surrounds us. Walt Disney was an incredible dreamer. But he didn't just decide to create his park because he found cheap land out in the middle of nowhere and had an important meeting with financial consultants who thought it would make him a great deal of money. No, he got his idea for an amusement park from spending time with his daughters on weekends. He wanted to create memories with his family and couldn't find anywhere in the world to take them to have fun and family time together.

In 2003, I got an idea after an imaginative conversation with my then nine-year-old son, Ryan. In October that year, Ryan was telling me how excited he was that our elves, Mr. Snoops, Mr. Jingles and Mr. Peeps would be coming soon on Thanksgiving Day and how much he had missed them. I told him that as excited as WE were for them to come, just imagine how THRILLING it must be throughout the ENTIRE North Pole on the night before Thanksgiving because ALL the elves are excited about leaving The North Pole to be with ALL the children ALL around the world! That sweet conversation led to a dream of creating a new family reading tradition to officially "Kick Off" the holiday season. In just a few days, our story, "The Night Before Thanksgiving... The Legend of The Christmas Elves" was complete and the new tradition was born—a tradition of gathering as a family on Thanksgiving Eve for a meaningful time of thankful reflection— connecting and sharing with each other moments for which we are grateful. Is my dream complete? Heck no! It is a continuous work in progress with much fun and adventure ahead!

What is YOUR dream? Dream the unbelievable, the utterly unthinkable, incredible dream...the wildly impossible, crazy, improbable DREAM!

— BELIEVE...
— Believe with all your heart!

"Have you ever believed in what sometimes seems like such a crazy goal? And have you wanted something so much that you ache deep within your heart and soul? Have you ever trusted FAITH to get you through those doubtful days? It just takes one step at a time, and soon you'll find that you can fly!!" These are more lyrics from my song, "Dream". We often say, "I'll believe it when I see it." But we need to believe it so that we DO see it. Again, Walt Disney truly believed in his dream of creating his amusement park. He believed in what he was creating so much that he wanted to let his close friend Art Linkletter in on the opportunity to invest in the land that surrounded what would be Disneyland.

As the story goes, Walt drove his good friend Art Linkletter to see some real estate property he had purchased. The two drove and drove for miles and miles until they finally drove off the main highway and down a small graveled road to see horses and cows grazing on a huge empty parcel of land. Finally, when Walt stopped the car and they got out, he began to describe, with great passion and excitement the wonderful things he wanted to build. He went on and on at great length and in extreme detail, describing his dream. He was ecstatic! Then he turned to his good friend Art, encouraging him to buy the property that surrounded this place. But Art was thinking to himself, the story goes … "who in the world is going to drive 25 miles for this crazy project? The logistics of the project are staggering!"

Walt continued, "I want you to have the first chance at the surrounding acreage, because in the next five years it will increase in value several hundred times." "What could I say? I knew he was wrong," Art said when telling the story later. "I knew that he had let this dream get the best of his common sense, so I mumbled something about a tight money situation, and promised I would look into the whole thing a little later on."

"A little longer will be too late." Walt cautioned Art as they walked back to the car. "You'd better move on it right now." And so, Art turned down the opportunity to buy the land that surrounded what was to become Disney Land. His friend, Walt Disney, tried to convince him, but Art thought him crazy! A few years later, Art served as the emcee for the opening day of his friend, Walt Disney's theme park, Disneyland. In the years to follow, Art would walk around Disneyland and sigh, "And there's another million I missed out on."

Believe in your dreams so you don't have any regrets. If you don't believe, who will? After I wrote my story back in 2003, I could have just left it right there on the paper and never moved forward with my dream. That is the easy route to take. It's easy to question yourself and your abilities:

- "Who am I to think I could start a new family tradition?"
- "Who am I to help accomplish their dreams?"
- "Who am I to …(fill in the blank)?"

If you believe in yourself and act on your dreams, others will believe in you and act to support your dreams.

Start right where you are and with the talents and resources you have. Don't wait for the "right time" or for your circumstances to change. Can anyone relate here, or am I just talking to myself? Look at the talents you have and what you can do now with what you DO have. When I wrote my first book, what I did NOT have was an office and a fancy publisher. What I DID have, however, was a huge, boxy computer sitting on the floor of my closet because … I didn't have an office. I would sit on the floor and type the copy for my story and website. Then when I started getting orders for my very "homespun" book, I would print the pages on sheets of paper with gold edges and staple them together with a red embossed cardstock cover finished off with a gold tassel. My dream continues to develop and expand, but if I had waited for the right circumstances to line up, like Walt Disney cautioned his friend Art, "A little longer will be too late." Believe in yourself and start NOW.

— BECOME…
— Become the shining STAR of who you are!

Everyone starts somewhere. There has to be a beginning date to someone's dream. But what does that look like? Are we highly successful the moment we begin working on our dreams? When a person or business celebrates an anniversary of the beginning of their dream, some people say, "I didn't realize they've been in business for 30 years," or "I can't believe that book has been out for 15 years." Many times it seems like everyone else but us is an overnight success. But if you look a little closer, you'll learn that every dream has a back-story and usually very humble beginnings.

Along the way, while continuing to sell my little "homespun" book, I started writing songs to accompany the experience. I was raising three young boys, supporting my husband in his career and cleaning houses for people to make some extra money to help support my dreams. While I was cleaning, I would hum, sing and think of new lyrics. What seemed like mundane actions involved in cleaning somehow stimulated my creativity and helped my dreams become a reality. One sweet lady I cleaned for in Mobile, AL would ask me to take a break and sing for her. When I sang for her the first song I ever wrote, "Dream", she actually gave me a $100 bill to help me be able to record it—and that's exactly what I did! Recording "Dream" was the beginning of taking additional steps to make my dreams a reality, which led to being invited to sing "Dream" at a national convention in St. Louis for 15,000 people—what a dream come true!! God bless my husband, Craig, along with family and friends who supported and encouraged me to press on. Because of them, this dream was truly BECOMING reality; and step by step, I was able to record all the songs in Nashville with J. Aaron Brown, a Grammy Award winning producer for children's music—another dream come true!

The next challenge ahead of me was to talk my sweet mother, Eva Manette Porter (Mimi), into illustrating the book. Mimi had always dreamed of illustrating a children's book, but the opportunity to pursue this dream had just never come about. She was an extremely talented artist, but didn't always believe in her abilities. I had to just INSIST that she do it! First of all, I told her that she HAD to illustrate it because I didn't have the money to pay someone to do it. Seriously though, I knew there would be no other artist but her to make this family legacy a reality. The "miracle" of Mimi's gift took shape and indeed, became another dream come true—for her and for me!!

Dreams coming true are simply dreams "BECOMING" truth!

As you think about your dreams, always remember this ... no matter who you are, no matter how old you may be, no matter your circumstance nor where you may live in this great big world ... you can always DREAM ... DREAM beyond the stars, BELIEVE with all your heart and BECOME the shining star of who you are ...

DREAM! ... BELIEVE! ... BECOME!

generationDREAM!

About Phyllis

Phyllis Porter Turner helps her clients to create a generationDREAM mentality – identifying their dreams, encouraging them to believe in their dreams and helping to make their dreams become a reality. Originally from Southwest Louisiana where tradition runs deep, Phyllis wrote the magical story, *The Night Before Thanksgiving... The Legend of The Christmas Elves*, which began a new family reading tradition serving as "THE Official Kickoff" of the holiday season.

In 2003, Phyllis had a talk with her then nine-year-old son, Ryan, about their Christmas elves, and what REALLY happens on the night before thanksgiving. This imaginative conversation led to her writing this story. Just as families hold dear to the "end all" tradition of reading *The Night Before Christmas* on Christmas Eve in anticipation of Santa's arrival. This 21st century holiday reading tradition is a way to BEGIN the holiday season with childlike wonder— ushering in the arrival of Santa's elves—year after year!

On Thanksgiving Eve, families gather for a meaningful time of thankful reflection—connecting and sharing with each other moments for which they are grateful, reading *The Night Before Thanksgiving...The Legend of The Christmas Elves* and dreaming of the wondrous days to come. This story and tradition are sure to be treasured for generations, as some of the most significant family traditions come from the simplest times of togetherness.

Phyllis' dream to create a movement of families adopting this heart-felt family tradition continues to grow. Since then, Phyllis has published three editions of the book and has also written and co-produced 12 songs with two-time Grammy Award winner, J. Aaron Brown of Nashville.

A graduate of McNeese University in Lake Charles, LA, Phyllis also studied at Belmont in Nashville, TN. She is the founder and creator of Elves Around The World and generationDREAM. Currently based out of the New York City and Philadelphia markets, Phyllis was honored to roll up her sleeves and work with the inaugural team of the new iconic FAO Schwarz Toy Store in Rockefeller Center, bringing wonder back to children and families all around the world.

Phyllis has worked with groups and individuals nationwide to encourage and inspire with her "DREAM" message —sharing the stage with motivational greats such as John Maxwell and Erik Weilhenmayer.

Find out how Phyllis can help you navigate your generationDREAM roadmap. She would love to send you a FREE download of her "DREAM" song for inspiration. All you have to do is connect with her at: Phyllis@ generationDREAM.com.

Have YOU ever had a dream?

DREAM! ... BELIEVE! ... BECOME!

generationDREAM

CHAPTER 5

SYSTEMS THINKING

BY DR. SAIDMUROD DAVLATOV

Success is not something you can achieve in a day or a night. Most often, this is the result of a carefully planned and implemented strategy. Success that comes too easily and quickly (for example, winning the lottery or receiving an inheritance) will pass from your life equally easily. True success is a combination of a number of correctly implemented actions.

Years of working in business have taught me to look at success as a human organism. A person is healthy when all the organs function in harmony. If, however, the functions of one organ are disrupted, the person feels pain. And a person does not die because all organs have failed at the same time. A person dies if any of their organs ceases to function properly, whether it is the intestines, lungs, heart, kidneys, liver, or stomach.

Success is like the human body. Since we cannot say that one organ is more important than another, it is impossible to single out any one area as being the most important. To achieve long-term and sustainable success, you need to take all components seriously, and there are many of them: a promising idea, a growing market, product choice, a close-knit team, market choice by geographical criteria, industry choice, a good strategy, a well-considered and consistent plan, and much more. However, all of this should be applied simultaneously. This is what I call SYSTEMS THINKING.

Systems thinking will help you realize many things that a conventional-thinking person would not see and achieve more significant results per unit of time. Nowadays, it is indicators such as speed and accuracy that are critical.

WHAT IS "SYSTEMS THINKING?"

1. You should make not one-time, but systemic solutions.

For example, you have a low income, and you decide to look for additional income or a side job. This is a one-time solution. If you build a business that will generate a constant, passive income, it will become a systemic solution. In other words, you make an effort once and then keep generating income.

Not so long ago, we held an annual meeting of our holding, and many people gathered in the office. It was winter, with snow, slush, and dirt outside. Walking along the corridor, I saw dirty footprints on the floor and asked the employees to wipe them away. However, the situation did not improve. People continued to enter and leave the office, bringing more and more dirt from the street.

I asked my employees to wipe the floor again. That evening, I thought about what a systemic solution could be for this situation, and, to start with, I looked at the work schedule of the cleaning lady. It turned out that she cleans the office three times a day: in the morning, at lunch, and in the evening.

However, when the weather was bad outside, and there were many people in the office, this was not enough. On such days, she should be cleaning all day long. This became the systemic solution.

Here's another example. You are constantly short of money. You have two ways to solve the problem. You can get a well-paid job and receive what we call a salary, and this is a one-time solution. Then, you'll have to keep on going to work to have money to satisfy all your needs.

However, there is another option. By doing what you do best, you can accumulate a small startup capital reserve and learn some skills. Using this capital and skills, you can generate a steady income for yourself and your family. This is called cash flow, or an example of a systemic solution to the problem. You make an effort once, and in the end you get a steady income.

If your business has low sales, and you are struggling with the problem through discounts and promotions—this is a one-time solution. A systemic solution would be to develop an effective sales system that will generate money on an increasing basis.

When you do not have enough money to develop a business, you borrow money or resort to loans. And this is also a one-time solution. However, if you create a product in demand and try to get income from increasing the sales of this product, this is a systemic solution.

When you learn how to think systemically, you will begin to search for and find a systemic solution to any problem, which means you get a better result with much less effort.

2. The effectiveness of your actions is determined by the ability to use the systemic approach.

For example, there are people whose one action gives only one result, while a single action of other people generates 10, 100, or 1,000 results. There are those who generate 100,000 results. And for a very few people, one action can generate even 1,000,000 or more results.

There are people who demonstrated their talent once and created a new medicine or a new promising product, and then this invention brings them a regular income for many years. You can achieve a similar result by developing systems thinking.

Why do you think some people make their dreams come true, while others do not? After all, people usually live for about 60 to 80 or 90 years, actively work until they are 60 to 65, some up to 70+.

Over these years, some manage to become billionaires, while others barely make ends meet. The time resource is the same for everyone: 24 hours in a day, 60 to 80 years of life. However, the result is completely different, and it all depends on whether people have systems-thinking skills.

3. Systems thinking helps build a complete picture from multiple parts.

By developing systems thinking, you can see how the people and resources that you need can achieve your goals, calculate how much money you need and where to find it, etc.

For all these components to work together efficiently and trouble free, systems thinking is essential.

I have long understood that if God gave you a dream, He will surely give you the resources, energy, willpower, and opportunities to make it come true. What you need to do is to develop your thinking to find these resources.

Systems thinking helps balance all aspects of your life: work, family, health, creativity, and the spiritual dimension. You need to perform the planned tasks and achieve results easily and without over-exerting yourself.

When you distribute the load evenly, you don't need to constantly motivate yourself to achieve results. You will practice the same action until it becomes automatic, and the habits formed will lead you to the goal without undue effort. In other words, we turn our actions into a system that helps overcome obstacles.

How does an athlete become a champion? They find the strength to do the same exercises every day—this is a systematic approach. Daily hard training forms a system, eventually transforming into a lifestyle, and this brings the athlete closer to fulfilling their ambition. And if, at first, they needed the willpower to work out consistently, then it is the systems thinking that helps them.

You can achieve great success if you develop systems thinking.

This is the *water drop strategy*. Water dripping day-by-day wears the hardest rock away. Rock is much harder, but the water will win all the same. **If you persist in performing the same actions that bring you closer to your goal, you can work wonders**. This will be a product of systems thinking.

4. Breakthrough point.

Systems thinking helps you find a breakthrough point. The other day, I was thinking about the fact that at any airport in the world we see the products of several world-famous companies, such as Chanel, Gucci, Kinder, Dolce & Gabbana, and Armani.

Bookstores around the world sell books by Napoleon Hill, Jack Canfield, Robert Kiyosaki, Brian Tracy, and other renowned authors. Video stores offer us movies produced by Hollywood film studios, like Paramount Pictures, Columbia

Pictures, and others. All cities in the world have sportswear shops, selling Adidas, Nike, and Puma goods.

This shows how important it is to find a breakthrough point in your business. Sometimes, you can do one right action instead of five years of laborious work. Robert Kiyosaki once said that he had used his own funds to publish his first would-be bestseller. After that, he took part in the Oprah Winfrey show, and sales of his books skyrocketed, reaching 20 million copies.

When Ray Kroc met the brothers Dick and Mac MacDonald, he immediately saw the McDonald's concept, which later turned his company into a thriving business empire.

Steve Jobs, visiting his friend and seeing how he transferred text on a screen by pressing buttons, realized that this invention had a promising future. As a result, the Apple brand is now known all over the world.

A systemic solution helps you see a breakthrough point in a business. My many years of experience in different markets made me realize that one targeted action can save 5–10 years of your life and leave the competition behind.

One of my businesses is perfume stores. I currently have 388. And my goal is to have 6,000 stores by 2025. My other perfume business, which I built in 2009, has 47 stores operating.

I woke up to the fact that *success is achieved not by someone who works hard but by someone who has found a breakthrough point in their business and regularly performs targeted actions in this direction*. Systematically analyzing and determining which actions have led to more positive results, they try to increase the number of those actions.

Using systems thinking, I determined all the effective actions, spelled them out, and formed a system for their regular repetition.

As a result, I now own 388 stores, and the system is developing without my involvement. Recently, at a meeting of partners, I thought about how much time I had spent building this company over the entire period of its existence. It turned out that it had taken me only two days, plus a quarterly strategic analysis of reports and adjustment of goals, which took several hours. Only four days in 2019! This is the result of systems thinking.

How I benefit from systems thinking.

In 2008, I had an incredible amount of debt: I owed money to 174 people and 4 banks, and my total debt amounted to $1,846,000 to individuals and $493,000 to banks. I worked very hard to repay the debts, but the more I tried, the faster the debts grew.

To pay off the debt, I took loans and invested in businesses, trying to achieve a stable income. However, after a year, I suddenly realized that I had more and more debts, partly because I had opened 36 sportswear stores but then had gone bankrupt and closed this business. For three years, I tried to implement 13 projects, and all of them ended up only with new debts.

My total debt increased to approximately $3,000,000. Then, I began to analyze my actions to find the efficiency point and set out my priorities. It was then that I stopped putting projects first and made myself a priority. I started working on myself more than on my business and considered the following:

1. How many hours a day I should read books.
2. How many hours I should spend attending specialized training courses.
3. What lifestyle I should have.
4. What habits I should build.
5. What support environment I should create.
6. How many hours I should devote to spiritual practice.
7. I wrote down all my life values and made a plan for their daily observance.
8. I formulated the basic rules for relations with my partners.

Until that moment, it seemed to me that by working on my business I could earn, repay my debts, and gradually become rich. *However, it turned out that the breakthrough point was not in my business growth, but in my personal growth.*

And after a while I noticed that I was gradually changing. My vision of my projects has become clearer, my plans more precise, my goals more specific, and my strategies more feasible. And this immediately led to positive changes in the business. I realized that the problem was not in the business, but that it was me who was a problem businessman who took on risky ideas.

By developing systems thinking, I realized that I had to use everything that made me stronger and brought me closer to the goal. It was harsh discipline in both financial and self-management that worked:

Systemic repetition of the same actions give the best result.

I realized that simply repaying debts would not allow me to think about anything other than these debts and all the arguments that went with them. Then, I developed a special debt repayment system and called it, "Debt melts away before your eyes." Now, it was not me who was thinking about how to repay debts but the system. And today, I have no debts, but the system continues to generate money. I reinvest and build new cash flows. I currently have 24 ongoing business projects. *It was a systemic solution to the debt problem.*

After I had repaid all my debts, my business started to grow. I was an investor, businessman, philanthropist, and lecturer, I did everything myself, and I was hard pressed for time. Then, I had to work on the development of systems thinking once again. I restructured the entire company and came to the idea of a new, holding business model. Now, the holding manages all the projects. This is an example of a systemic solution to important tasks:

A single action yields a million results.

Dear readers, in this chapter, I have shared my personal experience, and I hope that you can find something useful here to achieve your goals. The breakthrough point is in you, and the formula for success is the systems thinking. Here are my recommendations:

1. Spell out all your life values and a plan for their implementation.

2. Formulate your standards, move to a new level, and extend your reach. For example, to maintain good health, do 100 squats, 100 ab exercises, and 100 push-ups every day. Set yourself the goal of increasing your income by 20%–50% annually, and to save up part of your earnings (10%–30%) every month, etc.

3. Write down your life strategy, determine your life goals, and choose the most important ones. Find your growth point, your breakthrough point, invest time and effort in this direction. This approach will bring you positive results sooner. You can achieve everything if you can imagine it.

EVERYTHING IN YOUR LIFE APPEARS TWICE:

FIRST IN YOUR HEAD
AND THEN IN REALITY.

About Dr. Saidmurod Davlatov

Dr. Saidmurod Davlatov helps his clients become debt-free and reach financial stability in an average of 18 months. Using his own experience of climbing out of over $2,839,000 in debt in five years, he designed a unique system to escape financial bondage that he calls: "Debt melts away before your eyes."

The system helps people around the world with different incomes both secure financial stability and save money to start their own businesses – without the need for loans. What makes his system so special is that it functions entirely autonomously, creating a cash flow and paying off your debt – based on a pre-established schedule – all while you continue earning.

Thanks to his signature method of money management, more than 20,000 families have reached financial stability and no longer need to obsess over debt, loans and bankruptcy.

Dr. Saidmurod Davlatov is a speaker and globally-recognized business coach with more than 22 years of professional experience. He is a multimillionaire, investor and mentor. Throughout his career, he has had experience with 67 projects; currently he owns or co-owns 23 different types of business. He has more than 726,000 trainees, whose profits grow every year by 30% to 800%.

Over five years, Saidmurod has also taught individual courses to hundreds of businessmen, 292 to be exact, and coached 30 pupils who are now millionaires. The most successful one has earned $32,000,000 and is mentioned in Forbes magazine. He has spent over 2,000 hours in individual consulting sessions with entrepreneurs. Proof of their effectiveness is that 90% of his clients return for more coaching somewhere between three and eleven times.

As an invited speaker, Saidmurod has presented on the same stage as Nick Vujicic. He has given more than 200 speeches on TV and radio, and has published articles in newspapers and magazines. He is the author of the bestselling book, *Me and Money*, and the book series *Ant Philosophy*. His books have been translated into seven languages and sold over 2,000,000 copies. *Me and Money* is translated into English and has also been published in the USA.

He even created the "Me and Money" business board game that teaches money management before you even start earning, and developed the "Me and Money" mobile app to help you manage your savings in real time using his unique method. His own system of financial management earned him a PhD in economic development at the International Academic Accreditation and Certification Committee (IAACC) of UNESCO in 2015.

Currently, a movie titled *Mentor* is being filmed based on the real-life experiences of Dr. Saidmurod Davlatov. The movie is about a boy who was given over to a mentor when he was eight years old, but the civil war in Tajikistan in the mid-1990's forced him to move to Moscow and become a guest worker. It is a story of a man who, despite many obstacles, managed to find his purpose as a mentor, became a successful businessman and multi-millionaire, and taught others how to do the same.

To contact Dr. Saidmurod Davlatov, you can reach out to his promo director at the following email and website:
- karina.galoyan@davlatov.tj
- davlatov.tj

CHAPTER 6

IP ADDRESS UNKNOWN

BY CARAL RICHARD

The Internet Protocol (**IP**) is the method or protocol by which data is sent from one computer to another on the Internet. Each computer on the Internet has at least one **IP** address that uniquely identifies it from all other computers on the Internet.

Similarly, we all have at least one address that uniquely identifies where we live – a physical dwelling we called home. Our jobs, our church, our schools all have addresses that describe where they are located physically. But what about the non-physical? How or by what words do we use to describe the addresses of dwelling places where we also live but where they have no walls? I answer that question with a question.

What is the worst kind of prison? The worst kind of prison is an invisible prison, because if you can't see it, you will never see the need to escape from it. You will die as a prisoner, full of unused power, unspent riches and unrealized freedom.

I woke up this morning thinking about success and failure and the necessity of both. While in my pajamas, I went to the kitchen, grabbed some water and a banana and continued my contemplative journey as I sat on my sofa. I flipped on the TV and started channel surfing and stopped when I saw Supreme Court

Justice Clarence Thomas being interviewed on C-Span. He was talking about the differences between introverts and extroverts when I tuned in. I listened for 30 minutes as he described himself as an introvert along with a book that he was reading by author Susan Cain, titled: *The Power of Introverts in a World That Can't Stop Talking.*

When the interview ended, I picked up my phone, opened up Scribed, a book reading app and looked up the book Justice Thomas mentioned by Susan Cain. As I skimmed through the pages, I paused on a section where she was explaining the differences between Dr. Martin Luther King and Rosa Parks. Dr. King, an extrovert, was bold, dynamic and a masterful orator, while Rosa Parks, an introvert, was quiet and soft spoken, yet both were necessary to bring about powerful change.

I switched off the TV and closed the book reading app and stared at my half-eaten banana on the coffee table. Back to thinking about success and failure and why both are necessary. What makes one person great, and why do others fail? If it were just a matter of being positive all the time, then surely more people would be successful. Conversely, if it were just a matter of paying dues in terms of endless hardships, then undoubtedly more individuals would emerge with happier lives, right? What about desire? Wanting it bad enough? If that were the only prerequisite, most every person on earth who really wants a better, happier, more successful life in every way would have it. So where is the disconnect? Why do so many people struggle in vain to achieve their own land of promise? Why do most people fail and perish with outstretched hands toward freedom?

I believe it's because of what I call IP Address Unknown. Invisible Prison Unknown – so named because this prison has no walls, no shackles and no chains. There are no prison guards or barbed-wire fences. This prison is in our minds. It's our negative thoughts and destructive emotional patterns that are just beneath the threshold of our consciousness. We live unaware of their corrosive presence and silent bondage.

Negative thinking, self-sabotage, regret-thinking, victim thinking, jealousy, unforgiveness, entitlement, unwarranted fear, paranoia, selfishness, a worst-case scenario thinking-loop stuck in the 'Yes/But' syndrome. All of these disabling mental and emotional states are indeed invisible, but their bondage metes out life sentences to countless souls every day and ensnares more souls than all of the other physical prisons on earth combined.

THE GHOSTS AND CHAINS OF OUR PAST

I'd like to think that I was born happy. I've always felt a great welling up of joy on the inside of my heart regardless of the appearances in the physical world since the age of three. I am the grandson of share croppers, the son of a janitor and a mother who suffers from chronic illness. We were a middle-class Christian family living in Houston, TX. We didn't have a lot of money, but we were always clean and presentable – as was our home. But behind the scenes, there was a whole lot of fighting and yelling between my parents which often led to my sisters and I becoming the victims of their wrath in the forms of beatings. Back then, physical punishment was not only tolerated by authorities, but expected in order to discipline children. I remember in elementary school, sometimes after my classmates were paddled in the principal's office for bad behavior, their parents would be called and subsequently come up to the school and finish beating their child in the school office with a belt in front of a shocked crowd. I dreaded those beatings with a belt. They could come for any reason and at any time, and they did, so often.

While playing an intense game of backyard basketball one afternoon with my friends, my dad came home from work and demanded the basketball so he could take some free throws. I exclaimed to him that we were in the middle of a tie-breaker game, and to please let us finish our game first! You guessed it. He grabbed me and started beating me in front of all my friends. I could go on, but you get the idea. Why do I bring that up? It was one of the prison cells I lived in long after I left home for college.

Thoughts of regret and unforgiveness lingered in my heart for many years. When I got my acceptance letter and 4-year scholarship to the University at Austin, it was one of the happiest days of my life! I was finally physically free from the hands that caused me so much pain and suffering. No more beatings. No more listening to my parents argue. Happy ending right? Wrong. As a freshman student dealing with freshman butterflies, I was not aware how I would be affected from what I would now describe as PTSD. I couldn't understand why my mind would drift in class and began recounting humiliating instances of abuse or replaying scenes of yelling, crying and pain.

I wore my feelings of insecurity like a favorite jacket. Waves of emotions tossed me frequently between feelings of incompetence and low self-worth. I could go on and on, but you get the idea. I didn't comprehend why, despite all of my awards for outstanding achievements in school, why my self-esteem was in the dirt. That light, that awesome light of joy and happiness that had fueled me since I was a little boy was now flickering like a candle gasping for air. On some days it blew out completely.

Then, as a black male student at UT-Austin, I was not prepared for the racism I encountered there, though not all people are prejudiced. Thank God I had many genuine, loving white classmates and friends, but I never expected to exit a movie theatre after watching a movie with friends only to look down the barrel of a police officer's pistol telling me to freeze! Suddenly, me and my three black classmates were surrounded by an army of police cars; a few minutes later an ambulance pulled up and a white male student was rolled out on a stretcher. He was asked by the police, pointing to me, "Is this the guy?" Fortunately, he truthfully answered, "No."

Another time, while crossing 6th Street with a large group of students, the police summoned me away from the group and asked me if I knew that jay walking was illegal? Quizzically, I answered no, but quickly asked why were they not pulling the whole group of us over? My protest fell on deaf ears of course, and now I was arrested for disorderly conduct – as I watched all the white students continue to walk across the same path on 6th Street right in front of the officers.

I had never heard of the term "Racial Profiling" back then. Years later in Dallas, one day I had car trouble coming home from work. It was shortly after 5 pm. Dressed in a suit and tie, I left my car to walk to a nearby gas station to ask for help. A police car passed me and did a U-turn. Minutes later, I was in handcuffs because they said there had been burglaries in the area, and I fit the description of the suspect. I exclaimed, "The suspect wears a suit and tie and carries a brief case?" They replied, "Stop Resisting."

Ghosts that haunted me… remnants of my past… chains that no longer bind my wrists, but their imprint still embedded on my skin. Ghosts that haunt me – never quite there, never quite gone, always scary. Like the fictional character of Humpty Dumpty, all the preachers, teachers and friends, could not put Caral back together again. I was trapped in a prison that I couldn't see. I was in the grip of an iron fist that was colorless, odorless and 'addressless'.

Thank God for grace and mentors. My journey crossed paths with two earth angels named Garry Denning and Gene Madely. For reasons I will never understand, they took me under their wings, and through many hours, days, books and years of enlightenment, set me free from my old way of thinking. I finally realized that no matter how much I tried to become successful in life, my efforts would be futile unless and until I recognized this invisible prison and escaped. I realized that if I wanted to rise and reclaim my light, I would have to forgive the shortcomings of my past. Forgive my parents! Forgive the Police! Forgive the racist! Forgive my failures! AND Reclaim my confidence!

If there was one thing that I could say or point out that I've learned from my long psychological imprisonment in order to help someone else, it would be this: there is no one thing! There are only lots of small things that you must master over time. But this one thing I charge you to do ... ESCAPE! Find those invisible chains and cut them off. See your prison walls and plan your escape by forgiving those who hurt you or betrayed your trust or let you down. Read good books. Embrace good mentors. Only then can you truly experience the true freedom God has for your life. ... A life of economic power to go, to see, to do without limits as your heart desires. ... A life full of true happiness in all areas.

There is no one book or chapter that could capture my entire life story, but I no longer gasp for air like a flickering candle. I don't dwell in unhealthy negative mental states. I have risen from the drudgery of physical abuse and victimization to being invited to have dinner honoring our four past Republican Presidents Richard Nixon, Gerald Ford, Ronald Regan and George Bush Sr. as a guest. I've risen to work with clients such as Chevrolet and GM. I've owned my own brokerage firm and consulted with multimillion-dollar oil and gas companies, which include "thank you" letters from the late oil giant, T. Boone Pickens.

Use your negatives, use your failures as classroom lessons in life. Don't try to bury them. Don't blame yourself. Use them to fuel your inner candle power. Make sure that you break free from your disempowering past experiences and negative mental states through forgiveness. Both success and failure are needed.

- First – recognize what is your own invisible prison.
- Second – forgive and release your past failures but remember, there is no just one thing.
- Next – be prepared to rebuild your strength.

When muscles are not used over a long period of time they fall into disuse and lose strength. When you have been in the grip of mental and emotional negativity habitually over a long period of time, you must overcome the force of atrophy. The strength of your success mind and your success talk will have to be rebuilt gradually due to lack of use. Be patient as your strength to succeed grows. Make sure you consume a healthy daily diet of good books, both reading and listening to audiobooks. Surround yourself with beautiful mentors that will nurture and guide you back to the top of your mountain.

Once you have escaped from your invisible prison you must start building a fortress of power to repel any future attacks that may come to drag you back. And finally, live a life of gratitude. Be thankful for your illumination so that your candle power can intensify and glow like a star to serve as a beacon in the night for others.

Here's To Your Freedom....

About Caral

Caral Richard is the Executive Producer and CEO at Mobile Client Profits, a mobile marketing agency in Dallas, TX. There, he manages a talented team of highly-skilled digital experts and leverages his expertise as a Google Partners Specialist with 25 years of experience in Sales and Marketing to deliver exceptional results for his clients.

Caral attended one of the Nation's most prestigious High Schools for gifted and talented students, H.S.P.V.A in Houston, where he excelled and won numerous awards, including "Most Outstanding Musician" and "Most Promising Young Artist" Awards. Upon graduation in 1983, Caral received several scholarships and accepted a 4-year scholarship to The University of Texas at Austin. After two years, he moved to Denton to try out for the renowned One O'Clock Lab Band for Jazz, but before he could audition, he was told that he would have to retake academic classes already passed at UT-Austin before being granted admission to North Texas. Frustrated, he moved to Dallas and began his first professional corporate career as a licensed, registered broker selling investment securities.

Caral Richard quickly advanced up the corporate ladder over the next 6 years, eventually landing the position of Vice President of Marketing – supervising and providing ongoing training for over 40 brokers. He then struck out on his own to start his own brokerage firm, Crescent Financial and Crescent Energy, Inc.

After a 12-year career as an investment broker, Caral set out to start a new endeavor. As a former broker, he realized that his biggest clients owned car washes. With no prior experience, Caral launched Quick Pro Detail, a concept car detailing service catering to C Suite executives. He negotiated agreements with the largest commercial real estate management companies in Dallas to provide detailing services at the properties of Jones Lang LaSalle, CBRE (Coldwell Banker Richard Ellis), and Capstar Real Estate. The popularity and reputation of Quick Pro Detail quickly grew over the years, which lead to Mr. Richard landing clients like Ford Lincoln Mercury, Jaguar, Aston Martin, Chevy, Pontiac Buick and the largest car manufacture in the world, General Motors, to handle a portion of their car show exhibits in Texas.

In his spare time, he likes to hone his skills as a commercial real estate investor, jazz saxophonist, and Black Belt in Tae Kwon Do.

Contact information for Caral Richard:
- Website: www.MobileClientProfits.com
- Email: caral@mobileclientprofits.com

CHAPTER 7

BECOMING A POSITIVE THOUGHT WARRIOR
THE PATH TO GUARANTEED SUCCESS

BY DIANA COLE

In 2015, I was one month away from living in my car. My businesses were ailing, I couldn't pay my bills, and I often slept eighteen hours a day without ever feeling rested. I was losing my hair in handfuls, and I never felt good. I felt like worry and stress were killing me. I was internally desolate from years of betrayal and challenges, and I was only somewhat functional. Success was simply out of reach. Sometimes I thought it was close, but most of the time it was like a shadow in the night, painfully elusive.

For years I operated under the belief that if I worked hard and I was a good person, things would work out. I was not equipped for what I was experiencing at that point as a single mother and business owner. I felt like things were spinning out of control. I had my nose to the proverbial grindstone for a long time, until it got so bad that I finally admitted the truth to myself: *OK, enough! This is no longer for me.* I could see the life I wanted. I imagined it running concurrently with the life I was living but existing just above it. I wanted *that* version of my life, but I could not reach it.

I just couldn't make that leap up.

That's when I decided to change. If I could see it, I could live it!

Within months of making that decision, my businesses—which were not working—fell away and better solutions started appearing. Today, I am thriving, and I have found the success I only once dreamed of. How I turned everything around so quickly—and how you can too—is what this chapter is all about. If you are tired of feeling like success is out of reach, I will show you how to turn the tide—and I'll show you the truth: You have the power to live the life you want. And if your life is already going well and you simply want to know how to create more of what you want, I'll show you that, too.

One of my greatest passions today is teaching people the steps to have the success and happiness they truly want—*for real*. To claim their power. To get their energy back. To feel enthusiastic and optimistic about life again. To not settle for less than a joy-filled life.

While there is no secret pill, there are practices, exercises, and perspectives that are extremely effective when applied consistently. Each of the following steps will help to shake you free of your conditioning—free of limiting beliefs and perceptions that may have you waiting for the outside world to tell you whether you get to feel happy or not. Think about this for a moment: Almost every one of us have been allowing our circumstances to determine how we feel—and giving them all the credit. *I feel good because I got the raise or received the praise. I feel terrible because I failed, or someone doesn't like me. I feel amazing because he told me he loves me. I feel depressed because he said he's not ready to settle down.* But here is the radical truth:

Circumstances don't matter.

"Come on, Diana!" you may be saying right about now. But stay with me here. This is one of the single-most empowering truths I know:

To have true success you have to decide you're going to be happy <u>no matter what circumstance you're in</u>, and then watch what happens.

I'm not talking about a superficial happiness that is precariously held together by wishful thinking and a few glasses of Chardonnay. I'm talking about a real and abiding happiness that deepens with every passing year, an inner well-being that will carry you through life's challenging moments—a light than cannot be extinguished. This may seem like a tall order, but I promise you, this unconditional happiness can be yours. It starts when you begin to understand that while you can't control what other people say or do, you can control how you see things and what you say to yourself about them.

With the following four steps, I will show you how to become a Positive Thought Warrior—the most courageous version of yourself; the you who knows how to make life-changing choices and decisions. The you who knows that every time you fulfill one of your dreams, everyone else in your life wins, too. Your partner, your children, your friends, your colleagues, your whole world gets brighter when you feel strong and alive from the inside out.

<u>STEP 1</u>: Become Aware of Your Self-Talk

Becoming a Positive Thought Warrior requires that you first become aware of your inner world. The more you become aware of your self-talk, the underlying attitudes and beliefs fueling those private thoughts, and the feelings that they evoke, the more empowered and clear you become. The subtle power of awareness is astounding, really. It connects you with your unconditioned self and immediately begins to loosen the grip of old patterns of thinking and feeling. Ultimately, awareness allows you to choose thoughts that feel better.

When I first started working on myself, finding new ways to think about something (a condition or a feeling), was not easy for me because I had old patterns I tended to fall back on time and time again. Unwinding the knot of these patterns was not easy at first. If I started to think about something that didn't feel good, I focused on becoming aware of how I was talking to myself about it. I discovered that I had engaged in the same internal conversations many times before.

What are your internal conversations about? What do you say to yourself about you and the people you encounter? And what is the tone of your inner dialogue? Shining the light of self-honesty and awareness on the way you talk to yourself is a crucial first step.

<u>Step 2:</u> Enter Thought Rehab
I knew I needed to find better thoughts if I wanted to feel better. Starting with one positive thought would lead to a positive inner dialogue, and that would ultimately lead to feeling good. Since positive thoughts bring good feelings, I needed to stay in those positive thoughts for as long as possible. The trick was conjuring enough positive thoughts consistently enough to sustain a better feeling.

I surmised that I could easily and organically access positive thoughts by spending time doing what I like, doing what feels good. Doing what I enjoyed or what made me happy could start a stream of positive thought if I was conscious of the good feeling I was experiencing. In other words, I needed to be present in what I enjoyed and notice that I was enjoying it. It meant talking to myself about what lights me up and making mental observations about how lucky I was to be in that moment or experience. If I was consciously thinking about what made me happy, I could intentionally guide myself to come up with other positive observations when the organic thoughts slowed or stopped.

See what happens when you focus the power of your conscious intention in this way. When a negative interaction is in play, when negative self-talk arises, when a negative relationship pattern emerges, just stop. In the quiet that comes after the storm of negativity, listen deeply to yourself. Allowing that quality of listening will help you to step out of reactivity and habitual responses and show you what to do next.

Step 3: Create Positive Thought Chains
In order to keep my positive thoughts going for as long as possible, I needed to force it at first. I knew I needed to think conscious streams of positive thought and link more "like thoughts" to the original thought to form positive thought chains. I had to be conscious about it until these kinds of thoughts were my new normal, until I could think positively without even realizing it. The longer my positive thought chains the better I felt.

To create your own positive thought chains begin by noticing what you like. Then talk to yourself about it! The more you talk to yourself about what you like about your experience, the happier you will feel. Do this as often and for as long as possible.
As you do this, you'll find that in order to stay positive in thought, you'll have to think differently about the things you do not like. When you notice something you don't like, scan for something that feels good and choose to put your attention there. In this way, you're not in denial about what you don't like; you're simply not putting your energy in those directions. And as you talk to yourself about the good in every situation, you're building on your positive thought chains.

Step 4: Stop to Say Thank You
When you consistently ask the universe for what you want and it does not show up, think about the conversations you're

having with people and the conversations you are listening to. They are affecting your energy field. Like lint pulled from your clothes in a dryer, your wants and desires can be sucked away from you—disappearing into the socially acceptable trap of "harmless" gossip, petty remarks, and otherwise unproductive exchanges. In contrast, as a Positive Thought Warrior, you become a magnet that attracts your wants and desires to you.

You want to be in the same energy field or frequency with your real desires. Your desires are in a field of positive energy whenever you are thinking of them with positive expectancy, enthusiasm, warmth, excitement, gratitude, joy, love, or another high vibe feeling. When I got on my knees and thanked the universe for conditions that may have looked bad to someone else, it changed everything for me. I merged with the high frequencies where I feel most at home; most like myself. Almost instantly, I felt the warm rays of sunshine that create rainbows on rainy days, and I started to see rainbows all around me. My life was full of them! I realized that those rainbows were always there, I just wasn't focusing my attention on them.

I had been focused on the storms instead . . . and for too long. Although I could still feel when negativity or chaos would crop up around me, it did not affect me like it used to. It did not change my gratitude and appreciation. That's when I knew that I had made the leap up to the life I had always imagined.

What desires are alive in you that you can sync up with again? Are there desires that you've put away or lost touch with that would be uplifting to reclaim? And what part of your life would benefit from your appreciation and gratitude?

∽

Harnessing thoughts might feel like trying to tame a wild horse, but it is possible. You simply may need to draw on a little extra inner strength when you're making big changes or when you're faced with difficult situations or events. When I was stepping into my new life, I asked myself: *Diana, what do you most need to remember in order to have the success you want?* The answer boiled down to the essential lessons and directives that I know can serve you well along your own path to success:

o You are a miraculous human being. Remember to always stand tall in the face of challenge and opposition.

o Be happy now, *no matter what.* That means be happy even when things are not lining up with your desires and dreams—if you lose your job, are dealing with pain or illness, or experiencing a conflict with someone in your life. You cannot control conditions; you can only control how you perceive them—and how you dance with them. If your happiness is without condition, your success will be real, lasting, and profound.

o Don't wait. Thank the universe for your conditions now.

As powerful as thoughts are, you are more powerful than any single thought could ever be. In fact, I know for sure that you are powerful beyond belief. That's really the bottom line for all of us. We are not participants in our reality, we are creators of our reality. Understanding that power, responsibility, and freedom lie within us—that they are ours every time we choose them—is the way to guaranteed success.

About Diana

Diana Cole is a gifted intuitive, thought leader, and the author of the forthcoming book, *Spirit Translator: Seven Truths for Creating Well-Being and Connecting with Spirit.* An expert in the field of positive thought, Diana leads online courses and live events teaching people how to create lives of inner fulfillment and joy. As the daughter of a prominent figure in the New Age Movement in the San Francisco Bay Area, Diana's exposure to, and learning from, some of the most notable figures in the human potential movement is the foundation of her work.

Diana's early career as a fitness guru began as she desired to lead others out of pain. Through rehabilitation of her own back injury, she was inspired to teach the method she developed for becoming pain-free. As a successful entrepreneur, creating nationally-recognized brands in the fitness industry, Diana experienced a dramatic shift in her work and life when a series of transformative events led her to embrace the life-changing positive thought process she now teaches.

Today, through her spirit translation readings, she guides individuals and groups through the steps of connecting with their own spirit guides, and healing through positive thought work, she learned to live a happier life.

Her fast-growing Facebook community currently includes 1.2 million people. Diana and her family live in the San Francisco Bay Area.

CHAPTER 8

GOING THROUGH DARK NIGHTS

BY GRACE WANG

It was May 23, 1995. Carrying one suitcase, one handbag along with the American dream in my heart, I landed on American soil in San Francisco International airport by myself. Leaving everything behind, I stepped onto the promised land of the United States. After eight years of blood, sweat, and tears of preparation in China, working in the day and attending English class at night, saving every penny I could, my dream to see the outside world finally came true.

Without any time to look at such a stunning west coast city, I started working at a small jewelry store the very next day to feed myself and rent a room to stay. My excitement for the new world quickly vanished when I finally realized that I have to face the reality of uncertainty. I walked along the beautiful streets of San Francisco every night to ride the Bart (Bay Area Rapid Transit) home. It was always cold, wet, and rainy. I was drowned with a flood of loneliness and waves of homesickness. I was sad and could not find hope in this faraway dreamland. I saw a million lights from the buildings that surrounded me, like stars shining brightly, but not a single light belonged to me.

I still dislike San Francisco to this day, because whenever I go back, the intense feelings of despair return with it like a tornado, stirring up the feelings of sadness and hopelessness. It's a picture framed in my mind forever. Fortunately, my husband finally joined me one-and-a-half years later. His three attempts to get a visa were finally rewarded. He had the same nightmare almost every night for ten years, in finding himself denied the chance to reunite with me in the United States.

We started a new life in America. It began in the flea market, and we traveled to different cities and states to sell our merchandise. We sold everything we could get our hands on – such as gift items, jewelry, clothes, and toys – hoping to buy low and sell high. One day, we wandered around in the Salt Lake City fairgrounds of Utah. We stumbled on and discovered a way to make a living to sell everything in the state and county fairs. After five years of living in America, our first of two sons, Tyler, came into this world to join us, and two years later, Zach had followed. From our love of both food and avoiding the furious competition in selling merchandise, we shifted our business to become food concessionaires around the California Fairs.

Little did I know, the journey to becoming a food concessionaire was not only tough but also sometimes was like swimming in the raging waters. The first thing that a fair manager would ask, "show me a picture of your trailer and menu, then we can talk." Unfortunately, we could not afford the immaculate, fancy, custom-made food trailers. They usually cost anywhere from $300,000 to $800,000 for just one trailer. An additional RV to stay in during fairs would easily cost an extra $100,000 to $500,000, which even exceeded the cost of a single-family house where I currently live.

We decided to go for it. With the wildest imagination, along with my husband's handyman skills and my assistant beside him, from 2003, we began and built three fully-equipped food trailers by ourselves. From the design to building them, we worked day and night, and through the cold winter times. We poured our life savings and credit cards into making these food trailers as our American dream. One summer, we were finally accepted into three big fairs.

We set up at the three different cities and sold three different types of food. Mexican, Chinese and Sushi all at the same time. Life was beginning to look wonderful and hopeful. Our American dream seemed within inches of reach until it took a sharp turn.

We had hired many people to run the food trailers without supervision or proper training, and it turned out to be the biggest mistake we'd ever made. Without the efficient day-to-day operating system to run the food business, some people's integrity and honesty were tested.

Employees reported to me the stealing activities from food sales and neglected to follow the food procedure and regulation. One of our main food trailers was shut down by the local health department due to a violation of improper food handling. I had to drive 1,000 miles round trip from Southern California to Northern California without resting and sleeping to deal with these crises. My two sons were about three and six years old at the time, sleeping in the back seat of the car while I drove.

In addition to the chaos, we unknowingly hired a professional fraudster to run one of our food trailers. He claimed he injured himself only on the third day of work and threatened to sue. Our insurance company later found out that he had a record of more than three similar occurrences in the past. Before we knew it, we were deep in debt. Our credit cards were all maxed, we were only able to make the minimum payments, and our interest payments skyrocketed. And worst of all, we couldn't handle the fairs all at the same time at different locations. Businesses from fairs were not enough to cover the expenses. The concession spaces that we worked so hard to get, we now had to let slip before our eyes.

Our home mortgage was on a 5-year variable loan, and interest was increased every six months. Our house mortgage payment rose to our financial limit. We faced foreclosure on our home. In 2009, with no money to pay for the home we lived in and credit card payments due, we were forced to file bankruptcy.

Brain Tracy once said, "Life is just one crisis after another. We are either in a crisis or are on the way to a crisis." When the financial crisis hit our life, relationship strain came with it. My husband and I started blaming one another for all the past "bad" decisions. We argued and fought over everything and anything. Our bond and trust melted like ice out of the fridge. Our relationship was slowly sinking and on the brink of breaking. I had negative thoughts towards him about our marriage and the business decisions he made. A divorce crossed my mind many times, and very often during those difficult times.

Many nights I cried and prayed to God to point me in the right direction. I finally went to a marriage consultant for the first time in my life. I felt like my life was a roller coaster that now only went down. I was dropping into a dark hole and could find no way out.

I will never forget the day I finally woke up. A big and sudden wake-up call came to me. On a sunny afternoon, I spotted my two sons playing soccer on a huge fluffy and green grass field, laughing, chuckling, giggling, running and sweating. I looked at my two beautiful, incredibly talented and caring sons, and realized what was most important for my life. I had lost what I worked my tail off for so many years and yet, in the meantime, I was given those precious gifts and blessings with my family by my side. I was truly grateful and thankful that God gave me this opportunity to open my eyes.

I made a decision that day that there was nothing that could take my happiness away from me with my family ever again. The power of turning everything around was in my own hands. I felt revived. My sons were my heroes and saved me from going down the wrong path. I realized that I did not have any right to destroy our family, home, and future for what had happened in the past. If I truly loved my sons and family from the bottom of my heart, I had to face the challenges head on and find a way to work through the rough times with my husband.

Despite anything we experienced in the past, the future should be the only direction to which we should look. From that day forward, I madly started to learn from the best teachers I could find online and on radio – on relationships, communication and businesses. I read many books, watched countless transformational videos and TED talks, and took online courses on those topics. *The most profound secret I have discovered is that our minds are our most powerful tools.* We can create an entirely new and bright future by just thinking differently.

In 2014, I picked up a pen and began writing blogs. I shared my opinion and thoughts on relationships, business, and communication. Going through all my hardships had made me strong and humble. I discovered a passion that had been buried deep in my heart for so long. I found my treasure within me. Writing allowed me to live and cherish life again. I am now a popular blogger with a total of over 1.5 million readers. With the help of friends and family, I have become a successful business owner one more time.

The journey to pursue my American dreams has changed all aspects of my life for the better. I also rediscovered my soulmate and having a deep understanding about the meaning of love with my husband. Life has taught me that love, happiness and prosperity are choices. If I can change the feelings for the unpleasant things I experienced, I give the incident new meaning, and then I gain the power to create a wonderful future myself.

I have failed so many times along the way. And I know failures will come in the future as long as I continue to grow and want to be excellent at all the things about which I am passionate. I have learned that failures are good teachers. Instead of roadblocks, they are truly our milestones.

The year 2020 is so exciting and full of incredible possibilities. I hope my message not only can inspire you, but also transform you from where you are to a better position that you want for your life. If you want to keep growing and achieving your dreams, you cannot avoid failures. Never let the fear of failure stop you from winning.

Remember that the best wines with the most character and rich layers of flavor come from the grapes that went through the roughest weather.

About Grace

Grace Wang is a popular Chinese blogger with over 1.5 million readers. She is an entrepreneur and business owner. She is a freelance translator and writer. Grace worked as a food concessionaire for over 15 years, operated a restaurant for two years and taught cooking classes for two years.

Grace is a partner of "Empower Hour" – which helps women in need – a program that has reached over two million people in the United States.

She is currently a student of Jack Canfield, the world's best successful principle master, co-founder of "Storytelling For Success." In this group, she focuses on helping teenagers, parents, and entrepreneurs to become excellent communicators through dynamic storytelling.

Grace studied Accounting and English at American River College for five years.

She is a wife and a mother to two extraordinary teenage boys. Her passions also include photoshop picture editing and cooking.

You can contact Grace at:
- Website: MyHappyChoice.com
- Fiverr: Gracew2020
- Email: MyHappyChoice99@gmail.com

CHAPTER 9

LIVING YOUR TRUEST LIFE FROM WITHIN

BY DON NEVIASER

BE TRUE TO YOU

We all go through times of feeling socially unfulfilled or disconnected, and while seeking acceptance from others, may end up defining ourselves more through their eyes than through our own heart. Which can cause us to think and act more in line with how we assume they want us to be. Unfortunately, this can be in a manner unbefitting and untrue to who you really are. Plus you may not be accurately reading other peoples' thoughts and preferences.

Whatever your motivation may be, seeking approval and connection through submission or imitation, though flattering, will not genuinely connect or endear you very deeply or sincerely with anyone. Nor will it allow you to understand, trust and grow confident with your true self. It will also not give your heart what it ultimately needs and desires: solid emotional realities along with a variety of genuine, rewarding interactions with others – true relations that can only be enjoyed as a product of natural, real heartfelt connections.

Another thing to consider is that whatever your assumptions may be of how others perceive you, along with your subsequent actions and reactions, they may or may not be very accurate, valid or even necessary. Think about it; whatever your suppositions of their preferences may be, they are based on what they are saying, their actions and how you may be reading them. But what if you are misreading them? What if you are misinterpreting some or all of their words, actions and intentions in relation to you or others?

Or, what if they are being just as untrue to themselves and putting on their own show for the same insecurities and reasons? Either way, it is a bit ironic; seeking personal approval and acceptance from others by not acting like your true self. Alas, at times life can indeed be a stage.

But if your greatest desire is to honestly experience deeper and higher quality interactions and relations, try honestly acting and reacting in and to life, yourself and others, more faithful to the one person whose opinions and approval truly matters – and within whom your best happiness lies: you, your true self!

STEP UP FOR TRUE YOU!

Unfortunately for many people, even the smallest bumps on the road of life and pursuit can provide convenient excuses for giving up – especially involving actions or endeavors outside of common behavior. And a low self-esteem with limiting self-assumptions can, for some, justify living within a minimalist comfort zone of untested boundaries and self-imposed limitations. Thereby creating a general mindset that since they could never know proficiency, achievement or popularity beyond a certain point anyway, "so why even try?"

This also minimizes their actions and interactions with others. In fact, there are a variety of perceptions and beliefs that can keep some people unnecessarily locked in their own emotional prison.

This may be a very limiting, mental/emotional reality built with walls of negativity and self-discriminating thoughts and perceptions – lined with lost dreams, impossibility, wasted potential and minimal quality interactions within and with others – further sealing their door to a better life.

Living in a restricted life-bubble, or "hiding" behind walls of defense, can be further justified by the fact that it minimizes their chances of publicly failing at something and being embarrassed or ridiculed. A fear that, ironically, is many times based on past-botched attempts at accomplishing something that was actually the result of subconscious self-sabotage, follow-through and unintentionally confirming their assumed failure by actually making it happen.

Another reason that may minimize new efforts and accomplishment for some people is just not feeling deserving of success or positive experiences. Consequently, many great accomplishments, skills and incredible life-enhancing experiences and fulfillment will unfairly never be known by them. Unfortunately, by living such a minimally active life, they are also ignoring and throwing away so much potential, happiness, meaningful experiences and the incredible gift of life. And without a major self-perception upgrade, nothing will change.

However, the doors of possibility that lead to opportunity are, in fact, never completely shut. But the degree to which you are able to see, open and walk through them is directly proportional to how open your true heart and mind are to moving past assumed boundaries.

Even if you have regularly imposed self-assumed perimeters, you really can positively affect and improve your thoughts, perspectives, actions, reactions and life experiences on a daily basis. Through definitive choice and perceptual upgrade, you can raise your life bar and consistently improve your overall view of yourself, the quality of your life now, and your future potential for consistent, predictable happiness.

One of the greatest things about honestly opening your heart and mind to exploring and living your best life is that you will experience a far greater variety of rewarding life-enhancing experiences and pursuits – many of which you may not even know about. Honestly opening your true heart and mind also gives you the opportunity to continue exploring and growing your most creative and productive self. And in the process, not just enhancing your own life, but those of friends, family and others you will encounter on your journey.

In order to begin moving forward proactively and effectively, in line with your greatest self and experience true inner connection and peace, you must honestly and approvingly think, feel and act in line with your core person and innermost truth. And do so with nothing but genuine trust and faith. You, first and foremost, must be one of your best supporters! You have got to be there to approve of or validate yourself when you make mistakes or have doubts. And be a solid, supportive energy to help you continue rising up and pursuing your best life – the one you were gifted and deserve to enjoy!

Once you are genuinely self-connected, accepting of and aligned from within, you will be able to more comfortably think, feel and act from your true core. And you will be able to show the world, and yourself, who you really are, and can be, now and in the future, as you go on living a far more amazing life – one you really will enjoy.

A good way to begin supporting and exploring your best life is to first recognize the thoughts, feelings and perceptions representative of your inner truth and ultimate comfort zone, both latent and blatant. Once known, and believed, you can then begin to explore your innermost truths, needs and abilities – first to yourself for initial approval, and then honestly and comfortably to others. Granted, at times you may need an impartial validation from a trusted friend or family member to confirm you are pursuing something truly worthwhile. However, with or without that, whatever your past may be, you really are worthy of raising your life, and following your own best lead with genuine beliefs, actions and convictions. So stay strong and continue moving forward.

While opening up enough to pursue and enjoy more preferred experiences, you may also discover a variety of latent talents, abilities and unexplored aspirations – parts of your innermost true self and untapped potential that you never listened to beyond a certain point for lack of inner faith or ability to hear, believe or acknowledge them. Many aspirations of which may have been floundering in your heart since you were a kid. So, by open-mindedly looking deep within, exploring old and new desires, natural passions and intentions, without judgement, you will likely be able to further expand the doors of your true self. But just be sure to be honestly open, willing and able enough to actively perform and follow through on any new endeavors you may want to pursue. And only then, through real hands-on experience, will you know where some of your best inclinations of mental, emotional or physical rewards may lie.

While exploring a variety of new endeavors, you will continue opening new and unknown parts of your heart, mind and potential. You may also discover and enjoy a variety of experiences that could lead to other related, but unknown opportunities, depending on what you may be doing. The more openly you stretch your perspectives of heart and mind, the more you will expand your limitations and enjoy your best life! And you will continue discovering new and different personalized passions while experiencing a wider range of life-enhancing activities, both personally and professionally. But even if you fail at something, which everyone does now and then, take solace in gaining experience, and any potential new doors of pursuit you may have opened, that may be even more in line with your inner truth.

Actively searching for your greatest inner truth and potential is far better than continuing to deny your greatest happiness by not opening your heart and mind to a better, more expansive life. As an added bonus, while performing new and different activities, you will also meet and enjoy multi-faceted interactions and relations with different people and learn far more about your interactive needs and abilities – so you can also enjoy greater and deeper levels of multi-faceted connectivity and respect from yourself and others.

Granted, in the past you may have lived a somewhat limited life, focusing primarily on certain actions or efforts. And you may feel uncomfortable with experiencing a lot of new and different activities. But habits are formed through time and repetition. And in a relatively short period, your perceptions, thoughts and behaviors can and will comfortably change. And through some degree of consistency in action, new routines will quickly become comfortable and habitual, allowing you the opportunity to consistently grow, advance and expand your abilities and perspectives in many ways. And many past doubts of your potential, or fear of the unknown, will be replaced by new and better memories.

There may be times when you just feel overwhelmed or have doubts while pursuing and exploring your true self and most productive life. But, when that happens, try looking deep within, and honestly connecting with your innermost self with respect and approval – and acknowledge your relevant abilities now and future potential. Then continue mentally and physically stepping up to your plate of life and move above and beyond feeling limited.

Also keep in mind that though there is always potential for positive experiences and conclusions when trying new and different things, not every endeavor or interaction will run smoothly or be completely trouble-free. Whatever you may aspire to do, unforeseen problems or conflicts with others may arise – at times resulting in certain issues or barriers that will need to be worked through and moved beyond, if possible.

Generally speaking, a good, multi-faceted, successful career and life always involves effort, sacrifice and rewards – especially during times of trial and error, while vying for growth and success. Therefore, try mentally and emotionally preparing yourself in advance for a range of both potential or unpredictable, pertinent events and outcomes, both good and bad.

And whenever you do encounter obstacles or difficult situations, with the right mindset, efforts and follow through, a lot of challenges and resulting experiences can actually be great catalysts and opportunities for expansive self-discovery, mental and emotional growth or professional advancement. For it is only through genuine, hands-on experiences that your greatest resiliency, abilities and determination will be needed and well utilized.

And while pushing your boundaries, whether by solving additional problems or trying new actions and accomplishments, you will continue expanding and enhancing yourself and your skills. You will also learn more about who and what you really are capable of on many more levels, by bringing forth your best, most insightful and flexible self. And over time, as you continue expanding and enhancing your confidence and overall potential through different experiential lessons, you will be all the more successful both in and at life.

However your life and career may unfold, there will be both good and bad times and experiences. And sometimes you may not be as successful or rewarded as you intended. But whatever you may or may not have accomplished, owned or known, it will always be to your greatest overall advantage to create and honestly maintain a solid, daily attitude of gratitude, a heartwarming appreciation for you, your life as a whole and the many people and experiences that have, and will continue, enhancing, your life. Along with what you have achieved and how you will enhance the lives and happiness of others – further rewarding and expanding your inner image and self-esteem.

Another nice thing about maintaining a thankful mindset is that it helps minimize mental, emotional, and hence physical, energy loss. A positive overall attitude of appreciation also makes it easier to see the brighter side of things and infuse more positive perspectives and reactions, resulting in better end results, whatever you may be doing. And at the same time, many concerns, worries or people that may have reduced your joy and energy, or caused you pain in the past, will become less deserving of negatively affecting you mentally or emotionally beyond a certain point and wasting any more of your limited time and energy on.

Being more content and appreciative of you and your life, you will also want to share your positive energy and enhance the lives and happiness of others. But though you may affect them in a good way, you can only do so much to lighten their load. For them to truly appreciate and enjoy their own lives all the more, they, like you, must learn to deeply appreciate who and what they are through a solid realm of gratitude, gleaned from their own relative heart and mind-opening experiences.

But, if your own sense of gratitude is solid and true enough, it will genuinely shine into the hearts of others you connect with, even on different levels. And their perspectives will also be enhanced by seeing the true value and effects that gratitude can have on someone's heart, life and happiness. And as an added advantage of sharing real, positive energy and appreciation, especially during hard times for others, the more other people will genuinely be supportive of you when truly needed.

To further cement an attitude of gratitude, another perspective of thankfulness to consider is that, if you ever do take life for granted or are just feeling sorry for yourself, consider the fact that there have been, and are, millions of people around the world who would give anything to be where you are and experience just a portion of the freedom, good fortune and potential that you have. Even for just one chance to make at least some positive difference in their lives and the lives of their loved ones.

Maybe it is time to really believe what best defines not just who you would like to be, but accept and listen to who you genuinely are and can be. Then respect that real part of you and try to begin honestly and approvingly to walk in line with your greatest self and destiny – so you can live a life you really do deserve that is more in line with what your true self, and what your deepest heart really wants and needs to know, be and enjoy. Your life truly is something to be treasured and enjoyed! So, let your greatest inner life-light shine and live your greatest, most rewarding life...for however long it may be.

About Don

Don Neviaser has pursued a variety of careers, but deeply enjoyed being a certified Life Coach for 10 years. He specialized in helping people connect with their true self so they can live a life more in line with who they really are, and whether professionally, personally or socially, be able to connect with and enjoy more compatible friends, lovers and business associates.

Don is also an award-winning author. And because of his experiences in life, and life coaching, he has written several books on self-empowerment. One of his books, *The Power of Perspective and the Gift of Gratitude* won first place in the category of inspirational books in a national contest and was endorsed by Mark Victor Hansen. Currently, he is working on a major upgrade 2nd Edition of this book, *The Power of Perspective and the Gift of Gratitude.* The material in his chapter is from that book, which is being published by a subsidiary of Hay House Books, and should be available on Amazon.com and multiple other locations by early Fall of 2020.

CHAPTER 10

THE SECRETS TO LIVING A FANTASTIC LIFE
TWO SURVIVORS REVEAL THE GOLDEN PEARLS THEY'VE DISCOVERED

BY DR. ALLEN LYCKA & HARRIET TINKA

Dr. Allen Lycka is a speaker, trainer, author and respected former cosmetic dermatologist. His life collapsed when he suddenly developed a right foot drop in 2003. Soon after, his right arm became dysfunctional, and he was diagnosed with Lou Gehrig's disease (ALS) and given six months to live. Still, Dr. Lycka persisted and is here today as a result of his courage and determination. He is now a mentor, transformational speaker and thought leader.

Harriet Tinka is a former New York fashion model, a Woman of Distinction, and a youth instructor who endured being kidnapped, stabbed and left for dead. She is now a "Powerhouse Empowerment" expert who inspires audiences across North America.

Dr. Lycka met Harriet Tinka when she applied for a Woman of

Distinction Award that he was sponsoring for the YWCA. In large part because of their shared traumatic experiences, and their path to recovery, they became close friends. They wrote *The Secrets to Living a Fantastic Life* to share the key lessons to help readers find the golden pearls in their biggest challenges and make their lives fantastic too.

Dr. Lycka and Harriet Tinka have appeared on numerous TV and radio shows in the U.S. and Canada. Dr. Lycka is a TEDx speaker and a multi-time bLU talk speaker who has inspired audiences around the globe, and Harriet is an in-demand Public speaker and a Toastmaster Divisional Champion.

Read on to hear their stories.

DR. ALLEN LYCKA'S STORY

My life changed on a beautiful spring day in 2003. My wife, Lucie, and I had taken a holiday to enjoy a visit to Disneyland when Lucie turned to me and asked, "What's wrong with you, hon?"

I was confused. "What do you mean?" I asked.

My wife pointed out my right foot had suddenly and mysteriously developed a foot drop. It was audibly slapping on the pavement with each step.

My wife insisted, "When you get back, you need to get it checked out. "And you better listen," she emphasized.

All of a sudden, the happiest place on earth was not so happy.

So began my crisis. I sought out dozens of equally-perplexed specialists. They thought I might have a slipped disc or even developed a brain tumor. I commenced the million-dollar workup – every test known to man, CAT scans, MRI's, brain scans, scan scans. Guess what they showed? Absolutely nothing.

Then came the bombshell. One neurologist had me come to his office.

"You better sit down when I tell you this."

"Why, what's wrong?" I timidly asked.

"You have ALS (Lou Gehrig's disease) and you have six months to live. Get your affairs in order," he said.

"Is there a way to confirm the diagnosis?" I whispered.

"Yes," he said, "An Autopsy."

He had no bedside manner.

It's true that when your life is near the end, you see things clearly. You reach out. You look for answers. I rejected that diagnosis of ALS, as did my wife. "I don't know what you have, but it isn't ALS." she said. I began my odyssey to find an accurate diagnosis. I wasn't going down without a fight.

I went to the internet and searched thousands of sites. I stumbled upon the story of David Martz, a hematologist in Colorado Springs, Colorado. David had a story similar to mine, but he had deteriorated much more rapidly to be bed-ridden within months. He was on his death bed, barely able to lift his head from his pillow when his friend, a doctor from Texas, came to wish him goodbye.

What the Texan saw troubled him. He saw something that everyone had overlooked.

The Texan doctor dropped a bombshell.

He said, "David, I don't think you have ALS. You have Chronic Lyme Disease which is caused by a bite from a tick – resulting in a nerve dysfunction. If I'm right, you will recover rapidly."

The Texan doctor started David on a course of antibiotics, and like Lazarus, David miraculously arose from the dead.

Immediately after I read this, I knew I had to meet David in person.

I tracked down a phone number for David and placed the call. We chatted for some time, where David told me he had started a clinic treating people with this mysterious illness and during the call, he convinced me to fly to Colorado Springs, right away.

I flew the next morning, and I arrived half-dead. I went through the worse storm imaginable. I crawled off the plane. David immediately met me on the tarmac, hugged me, and brought me to his office. He confirmed I had Chronic Lyme Disease and started me on treatment. It stabilized my illness and it's the reason I'm alive over 15 years after I was supposed to die.

Ever since, I've been living on borrowed time. That's when I had a second chance to live more abundantly. And although I had been afflicted, I had been blessed. I finally knew God's plan for me. I could help others find solutions for their problems, just as I have done, without the hardship or difficulty I had encountered.

HARRIET TINKA'S STORY

I was hobbling slowly on crutches in the hospital hallway towards the waiting room. I was wrapped up in what the hospital staff called the "Johnny Gown." This gown left me partially exposed to strangers and undermined my dignity. "What a stupid invention," I thought. I had no control of my life anymore: a prisoner wearing a Johnny Gown and a wristband with a serial number.

As I sat down, I could hear voices in agony in the examining room. It was strangely comforting to know that others were also fighting their own demons. A squeaky noise diverted my attention. A joyful little girl was piloting herself in a wheelchair.

I wanted to be alone. I made no eye contact hoping she would continue wheeling herself past the waiting room.

"What's your name?" she asked as she slowed down.

"My name is Harriet," I answered irritably.

"I am Amber, and I am nine years old. What are you doing here?" she asked.

"I am here for physical therapy for my injured leg," I responded.

"You have crutches. What happened to you?" Amber asked.

I thought back...

REWIND TO HARRIET'S TRAUMA

I was a young teen at 5'8", 110 pounds, working as a fashion model in New York City. I was chosen because they said I was beautiful. The industry was supposed to be glamorous, but, in reality, it was cut-throat. I learned to embrace rejection. The experience ranged from harsh criticisms, false flattery and starvation to magazine photo-shoots, fashion week tributes, and modeling gigs in a dozen countries.

After surviving ten years in this hypocritical industry, I decided to leave and get a formal education. I enrolled as a student at the University of Calgary in Accounting. The university was happily three hours away from my family – far enough away to be independent yet close enough for help, if I needed any.

Though outwardly I was popular, inside, I felt alone and vulnerable. I made a few friends, amongst whom Martin was one. He was charming, witty, thickset, short, and older than I was. Martin was an introvert with few friends. I was happy because Martin was fond of me. But he soon revealed a dark side of himself. He was fiercely jealous with the times I spent with others. He was manipulative, bad-tempered, and threatening. Unbeknownst to me, at that time he was a sociopath.

He isolated me from my friends and started stalking me. I had safety concerns and his actions went to the point where a restraining order was issued. I thought it was over.

One Monday night, I stayed late at the university and walked home. I stepped into the elevator, distracted because I was fishing through my handbag for keys. Suddenly, somebody grabbed my neck from behind. I was frozen with fear.

"You thought you could escape me?" a voice whispered in my ear.

It was Martin. The restraining order meant nothing to him. His hands reached up quickly and squeezed my neck tightly as I gasped for air. I heard voices coming from the building. I tried to scream, but he turned me around and hit me in the stomach. He took out a butcher's knife from his pocket and placed it in front of me to silence me.

"You know I am the only one who could ever love you unconditionally," he shouted.

Then he sliced my right-hand middle finger. Blood poured from my finger onto the floor of the elevator. He covered my mouth, dragged me out by my hair, bashed my head on the car, and threw me inside. I was in so much pain.

Martin drove recklessly into a nearby car dealership. He stopped and seized a baseball bat from the back seat and began smashing the car windshields. After this display of uncontrolled rage and intimidation, he drove for some time, ending at an isolated area west of the city. There, off a roadside turn out, was a highway phone booth. He commanded me to call my family to bid them farewell. It would be the last time they would ever hear from me. Timidly, I refused the first time.

In anger, he told me, "I have a rope, a knife, gasoline, and a gun. I am going to tie your body with the rope, cut you in pieces, and spill gasoline all over you. Nobody will ever find you. Now, will you call them?"

Somewhere, I still found the courage to refuse.

In a flash, he stabbed me twice in my left thigh. I screamed from the excruciating pain as blood gushed onto the windshield. I lost consciousness. Martin ran out and left me to die.

I never found out how I got to the hospital. I opened my eyes. The police and my father were at my bedside. My father had driven for three hours that night to be with me. He felt powerless.

I felt shame. I blamed myself.

MY HEALING PROCESS

My new challenge was to learn to walk again using crutches. I was once a runaway model, now a cripple, in a Johnny Gown.

The irony is that the court gave my abuser only three months in jail for attempted murder.

I fell into a deep depression. I would cry silently, with the belief there was no one to help me. I was a failure. Determined to end my life, I swallowed a full bottle of sleeping pills and went to sleep. I woke up disorientated. Even trying to end my life was another failure.

Amber drew me out of my slumber. She shared her story with me. Amber was an only child. A drunk driver ran a red light and struck their vehicle, instantly killing both her parents. She was now motherless, fatherless, homeless, and paralyzed from the waist down. Yet, filled with joy and happiness. I asked her how she exuded joy after enduring such a tragedy.

She looked at me with a sincere smile and whispered, "I am lucky to be alive. And you're alive too. Maybe you can use what happened to you to make changes in the world. I know I want to."

This crippled nine-year-old girl was the catalyst, my call to action.

MY FANTASTIC LIFE

I needed to meet Amber to find my purpose. The trauma taught me that one cannot expect a perfect life and must appreciate that moments of beauty will be interspersed with tragedy. I have learned to forgive. The hardships made me stronger. I learned it was not what happens to you, but what you do with what happens that is important.

Harriet: Dr. Lycka, we have shared our personal stories with our readers. We have come through some pretty horrific experiences. Dr. Lycka: But like steel, we were tempered by them. We survived and used our experiences as "turning points", learning how to live fantastic lives. And because we survived, we discovered "13 Golden Pearls" that will help others live fantastic lives too. Can you share a few of your favorites?

Harriet: That'll be hard because I love them all, but I will give it a try. Here they are:

1. Attitude – David Goggins, a retired United States Navy SEAL, who distinguished himself as an ultra-marathoner (a passion I share) stated: "Attitude is absolutely everything in life! The only thing more contagious than a good attitude is a bad one." I believe that as well.

2. Intention – Ellen DeGeneres said, "I believe we're all put on this planet for a purpose, and we all have a different purpose... When you connect with that love and that compassion, that's when everything unfolds." Hence, this is my second favorite pearl.

3. Empowerment – Nora Ephron said, "Above all, be the heroine of your life, not the victim."

Those are my three favorite golden pearls. What's your favorite pearl, Dr. Lycka?

Dr. Lycka: It's enthusiasm. Let me share a story about that.

It was a cold November day. Fred, the carpenter, was tired. He had worked 35 years for his boss but could not rustle up any more enthusiasm to do so. So, he went to his boss and said, "It's time for me to quit."

His boss thought about it for a moment. He said, "Before you quit, can you do one more job for me? I need a special house built and you are the only one I'd trust to do it."

Begrudgingly, Fred said yes. But he had no enthusiasm. He got to work late and left early. His work was barely passable. So bad in fact, that when the house was done, it barely passed inspection.

When he was done, Fred delivered the keys on his boss's desk. Fred said, "Ok, I'm done".

The boss said, "Not so fast." He called all the employees together.

"Everyone, this is Fred's last day. He has been my loyal employee for 30 years. Now I have a special surprise for Fred. For the last year, Fred has been involved in a very special project. He has built me one last house. Now, today, I am giving him this house. Fred, I hope you enjoy this in your retirement."

Here's the motto:

BRING YOUR ENTHUSIASM EVERY DAY

And that's why this is my favorite pearl.

About Dr. Allen Lycka

Dr. Allen Lycka is acknowledged as one of the most respected cosmetic dermatologists in the world. Having practiced for three decades, he has helped tens of thousands of patients. In Edmonton since 1979, he's written 17 books, 30+ academic papers and hosted the number one internet radio shows on cosmetic surgery – *Inside Cosmetic Surgery Today.* He is co-founder of Doctors for the Practice of Safe and Ethical Aesthetic Medicine.

Dr. Lycka has been acknowledged by his community by awarding him the prestigious Consumers Choice Award for 16 consecutive years and the Philanthropist of The Year award for 2013.

Dr. Lycka is happily married to Dr. Bernier-Lycka for 38 years, and they have four wonderful daughters and seven beautiful grandchildren. He counts these as his most important accomplishments.

About Harriet

As a Turning Point expert, Harriet Tinka, CMA, CPA, CCP is a perfect example of someone finding a need in the community and filling it. Despite dealing with obstacles in her life, she has overcome those hurdles and has found success by inspiring thousands of audience members to reach their full potential. She was stabbed, kidnapped and left for dead. She turned that horrifying experience into motivation. She has inspired and given hope to women who are faced with domestic violence. She is known by her students as a "Powerhouse Role Model" who makes being genuine the most powerful thing of all.

- Harriet is an invigorating transformational speaker, passionate life coach, blogger, Chartered Professional Accountant, Football Official, and an ultra-marathon runner. She is the founder and CEO of the award-winning Social Enterprise, Empowered Me Inc., a company whose mission is to inspire and empower girls and women.

- Harriet has received numerous awards, including YWCA Woman of Distinction, Global Woman of Vision, Afro-Canadian Community Woman of the Year, Action for Healthy Communities Youth Empowerment Award, Rotary Integrity Award and Daughter's Day Award just to mention a few. She is a tireless philanthropist, and a Toastmaster Divisional Champion.

- Harriet feels blessed to have her journey supported by her partner Steve, and her three lovable children: Tristan, Rhiannah and Aaliyah.

CHAPTER 11

APPLY NATURE'S WAY
LEARNING TO FLOW

BY JACOB MOYA

My contribution is to a topic that is fascinating and barely explored, but one that can easily define how easy or difficult your road to success, in the area you are looking to improve, can be. It is important to learn and understand how nature works because we are all part of it, and we are following certain natural principles all the time. Understanding them can cut down dramatically on the time it is going to take you to get to the place you want to be in the areas of love, health and money. Are you in receiving or in rejecting mode?

THE LAW OF BALANCE

The third dimension, or our physical life, is characterized by our search for balance at all times. Everything around us is ruled by this principle in one way or another. Balance is everywhere! It is inside and outside of you. Winter is balanced by summer, fall balanced by spring; day by night; the North Pole balanced by the South Pole, the sun by the moon; men by women; and children by elders. Inside our bodies, we have male energies and female energies, our right and our left side, what we like and what we don't, what we love and what hurts us, pleasure and pain, and—

if we take it deeper—our physical experience balanced by our spiritual experience: someone needs to die in order for someone else to live. Someone needs to be sad for someone else to be happy, someone needs to be healthy and someone else needs to be sick.

This dance goes on continuously, all around us, and throughout our days. Sometimes during the day, we can be happy and then suddenly we can be melancholic or even sad, or jump from feeling good to being sick in a matter of hours. Consider the *Law of Balance* when you are building your new venture, and especially when you are choosing people to work with.

The days of a month also go through a cycle of balance, from the emotional aspect during a full moon that supports all emotional connections and introspection, to the physical cycle of the new moon that supports new ventures, goal setting, contracts, and physical plans. Do yourself a favor and avoid starting a business or making transformative decisions three days before the full moon, on the day of the full moon or for three days after. If you are in a relationship and you feel disconnected from your partner during this period, use it as an opportunity to get closer and have open-hearted, vulnerable conversations, not to break up or take a break, please!

What's the lesson here? Time your plans and decisions. Don't fight the world's natural energies, flow with them!

OUR BRAIN

Your brain is part of your physical body, and acts like the big brother who is in charge while you are here in the world of the living. Your energetic/emotional and spiritual bodies are like twin younger brothers. What you do to one affects the other, but they are always at the mercy of the choices and decisions of their big brother, your physical and logical brain. The two other bodies may influence and suggest choices (hunches), but the one in charge is your brain, which is very shortsighted. It can only assume things based on events that it has already experienced. Everything else gets dismissed as non-possible or non-existent.

Your physical life is very important at a spiritual level, because it is finite. We are all here to experience certain physical things and emotions in a fairly short time. We have the gender, race, skin color, size, shape, age, parents, siblings, friends, health and wealth to either balance a previous life experience or to allow us to experience certain emotions that will help our spiritual growth and development. Therefore, everything starts and finishes with your intention. If you do not create the intention to experience something, you are not giving permission to all the unseen forces to help you and guide you towards your desired goal. The forces assume that it is important for you to live the experience that your mind is choosing to have at the moment, and they respect that. After all, you can always come back and try again.

We humans are also programmed to miss or desire what we don't have. That's the primary component that allowed us to evolve, but it is always rebalancing naturally, according to the *Law of Balance*. And then we have the mighty and misunderstood subconscious mind. This is the place in the brain where we record our very own rules for how to live our lives. It is a composite of all the emotional reactions to physical experiences that we have lived or witnessed since we were in our moms' wombs. When we go through deep, emotionally-charged experiences, this part of the brain opens up and records the events and reasoned rules in real time.

When all your senses are activated and your dopamine and endorphins are triggered, the recording starts, and whatever logical reason you credited for the experience you are having will create a trigger, a reference point or a new life rule. This trigger will produce a physical, chemical, and emotional reaction every time you hear, smell, feel or see any of the components that were present when that recorded event was originally placed in there.

Of course, the judgment or outcome you recorded there, will be assumed to be the expected result of your current experience, even if the players are different or you are consciously choosing to go and experience this new event.

Your subconscious is so powerful that it will block everything that doesn't match, or that would allow you to have an outcome different from the one previously recorded, from your sight and reason. It is very easy to see this at play in relationships. When you are in one, you miss the freedom of being single, and when you are not in one, you miss the companionship and love of one. This happens, like I mentioned before, not only because we miss what we don't have, but also because of our previous painful experiences reference points.

So be very careful with self-dialogues when you are angry, under stress, hurt, or in physical pain. Use the opportunity to record the information that will serve you in the future. For example, cry all you want after a painful breakup, but say to yourself, "How beautiful it is that I could love someone this deeply, and that (he, she) allowed me to find someone capable of loving me back with the same intensity." It is totally forbidden to call yourself stupid or pass to any other judgment like "I was better off single" or "I should know better."

OUR LIFE CYCLES

We all go through three different major cycles during our lifetimes. These cycles match the three groups of internal energy centers in our bodies. The first third of our lives is all about the _physical experience_ and corresponds to the group of three lower energy centers or chakras. We then shift to our _balanced life cycle_, which corresponds to our heart or middle energy center, your heart chakra. Lastly, we move to the final third of our lives, our _enlightenment cycle_, which usually runs till we die that corresponds to our three top energy centers or chakras. Life would be very easy if we only had or experienced our major cycles, but it is not like that. During each major cycle, we also have mini- and micro-cycles that take us from one extreme to the other, but that always respect the influence of our major cycle. Let me give you an example of this. As children, we learn the concept of God and spirituality as a physical form, we develop a concept of good and bad based on what we actually want at the moment, and we love and hate our parents or guardians based on how they meet our needs. As adults, we tend to adjust the concepts of religion and love to suit our new way of thinking, and this is especially noticeable in the way we feel towards our parents or guardians. These concepts totally shift when we become parents, adopt pets or experience the deaths of love ones. Physical things become important—how we look, what others think of us, and so on. Then, in the last third of our lives, after we have experienced disappointments and a few setbacks, we tend to understand that what it is important is our health, experiences and the love exchanged between the people we learn to love or our family. At this time in our lives, regrets usually set in, and we spend a good amount of time contemplating and enjoying the simpler things. Our connection with our spiritual beliefs rises in priority.

When you are in an inner growth cycle, usually all material things go bad! You make the wrong financial or business decisions, your clients cancel your contracts or appointments, it is hard to collect on past invoices, you cannot find new clients or prospects no matter how hard you try, you just finish paying something off and something else breaks, or you get sick, etc.! But to balance this experience out, you connect easily with people around you, and your friends call you and pay special attention to you. If you are single, other single people suddenly notice you. If you are in a relationship, your partner tries to cheer you up and try to get emotionally closer to you. You start caring for stuff that is more meaningful and less trivial, like health instead of material things, learning instead of watching a TV show or a movie, and so on.

Now, everything would work amazingly well if we could only

be aware of the cycles and ride the wave, but we also have the *Law of Polarity* embedded in our programming, remember? We want what we lack! And we do it naturally, without being aware of it. We waste our season to regroup and acquire new skills by crashing over and over, trying to make our businesses, careers, or our financial wealth grow. If you are stubborn enough, you will manage to get away with it, but when that cycle finishes and you transition to the next one, you will be drained, emotionally disconnected from people who care for you and your well-being, and without the new skills, knowledge or relationships to take full advantage of your new physical cycle.

I will strongly suggest that those of you who are building a business, and it is time to bring in a helping hand or someone who will have a saying in the hiring process, to invest a little bit of time and money to find out which *major cycle* your prospects are in and when their cycles will shift, with a Numerologist or an Astrologer. Another thing that is very important for you to consider is *your current major cycle* and when that will shift, so you can match it to that of your prospected employee. Just imagine how challenging it can be to work with someone who is talented, but who has almost everything they do go bad.

I also strongly recommend that you take a few minutes now and review your story to find pinnacle moments in your life and try to determine which cycle you were in before, during and after those moments. Learning to read the signs will help you to find which cycle you are in at the moment, and accepting it once you do. This practice will lower your stress to a manageable level, and will therefore improve your health, your relationships, your communication with others, and your understanding of and respect for others. With patience and practice, you will eventually learn how to flow in your life instead of fighting your way through. You will be aware that you get what you need and not what you want, and it is a blessing that life works that way! In other words,

EVERYTHING HAPPENS FOR YOUR OWN GOOD!

Notice how we need to get sick before we develop the antibodies to successfully resist and fight future imbalances in our bodies, how we have to exercise and eat properly to be healthy and on the slimmer side, how we need to avoid spending more than we earn in order to have savings, take chances with our hard-earned money in order to have investments, go to school to get the skills that produce an income, etc. It has always been that way and will continue to be that way, so try to remember that EVERY TIME you are going through a challenge. Reframe it to "I'm back to the school of life; it's time to learn something or to connect with someone that was not originally on my path, it is a very important time; thank you Lord, Jesus, life, universe, higher-self," or whatever you believe in, and flow!

Don't fight the challenges in your life. Embrace them and take notice of everything that you are forced to live and experience because of them, no matter how long your cycles last. Everything was supposed to help your journey, anyway.

About Jacob

Jacob Moya helps his clients to remove and heal all emotional and energetic blockages by healing childhood trauma, karma, and eliminating permanently emotional cords and attachments that prevents them from experiencing a fulfilling, harmonious and healthy life.

He is the creator of a new therapy modality that helps his clients' bodies to fast track the release of the emotional or energetic blockages, to bring them back to balance and recovery mode.

He grew up in Mexico City in a fairly unusual family. His siblings and other relatives had natural abilities and were awakened since they were born. He was an empath Indigo child in times where the only support system was the Montessori educational system. He is dyslexic. He was exposed at a very young age to many different forms of organized religion, prayer houses, an ashram and self-study programs. At 26 years old, married to his first wife and with his only newborn daughter, his aunt, who had learned how to control her natural channeling abilities, taught him and his younger sister to channel. His natural introspection and fascination for finding answers while practicing deep meditation channeling, took him deeper and deeper into healing and onto a spiritual path.

He also worked in the mainstream world. He was a successful life insurance agent, mortgage broker and check-cashing store owner. At the end of 2014, He followed an inner hunch and started a new journey, and got certified in hypnosis, NLP, energy psychology, energy medicine, Paida-Lajin and other self-healing modalities that gave form and structure to his already-known spiritual wisdom. He has his own in-person and by-phone practice where he uses his self-developed system that respects clients' natural energetic flow to help them heal their physical and spiritual scars.

He has active clients in many cities of the US, Canada, Mexico, Brazil, Argentina, London, Ireland, Scotland, Jordan, and Barcelona.

You can connect with Jacob at:
- JMoya@Heal2Flow.com
- www.facebook.com/AncientWisdomInstitute

CHAPTER 12

PUT YOURSELF IN THE DRIVER'S SEAT: CREATING A PERSONA OF IMPACT

BY NICK NANTON & JW DICKS

Al Gore was supposed to be a sure thing.

In January of 2000, Gore was coming off serving as the Vice President in the popular two-term presidency of Bill Clinton, who still enjoyed over a 60% approval rating despite the Monica Lewinsky scandal. The economy was in great shape and there was no reason to see trouble for Gore, who was running to replace his boss.

Except some Democrats still did...

Throughout his career, Gore's public appearances were tagged with words like "wooden," "pedantic" and "boring." Clinton's charm and charisma, of course, completely overshadowed Gore during their 1992 and 1996 runs, but Gore, in turn, was important for adding some stolid stability to the freewheeling Clinton campaign.

But stolid stability wasn't the most wonderful asset when it came to running for President in the age of the media masters like Clinton. Voters wanted someone who could make them feel good and command their attention—and Gore would be hard-pressed to deliver that kind of excitement in the run-up to November.

That's why, exactly one year earlier in November of 1999 as Gore was gearing up for his run, feminist Naomi Wolf was hired to help transform him into an "alpha male." She advised him on wardrobe and attitude and charged the campaign $15k a month for her services. The problem was, *Time* magazine found out and printed the story, which made Gore look ridiculous from the outset.

And then came the debates.

In the first debate, most observers thought Gore came across as more knowledgeable and nuanced than Bush. However, most observers also thought Gore acted really, really weird. When Bush answered a question, Gore would contort his face and sigh loudly or roll his eyes, like he was in a silent film comedy. The sketch show *Saturday Night Live* viciously made fun of his tactics. In the second debate, Gore seemed to learn his lesson and stop over-acting. Unfortunately, he just appeared as the wooden bore his handlers were afraid he would be.

Then came the third debate and the strangest Al Gore moment of the campaign. After Bush answered a question, Gore walked away from his podium and towards Bush, stopping a few feet away from him and glaring at him silently.

Bush merely turned towards the Vice President, gave him a preemptive nod, and turned back to the audience.

Even though many thought Gore's command of the issues was far greater than Bush's, people were left feeling uncomfortable about the VP. One woman summed it all up by saying, "He had a different persona in every debate." All of which resulted in a close election nobody thought would be close, and George W.

Bush becoming the next President of the United States instead of Al Gore.

In this age, every successful politician has to be what we call a "MediaMaster," someone whose *personal persona* must connect with the voters in order to triumph at the ballot box. And the same goes for most successful entrepreneurs.

In this chapter, you're going to learn what we believe is a key pillar of success: Crafting a Persona of Impact so you can conquer your niche and draw the most loyal, fervent following possible.

What is a Persona of Impact? It's a personality-based style of communication that goes beyond the universal basics, built specifically on *who you are* and your *distinct personal qualities*. It's great to become as polished and professional as possible in your media presentations. However, if you don't also create your own *individual* appeal, your audience will have difficulty truly bonding with you as a person – especially if, like Al Gore did in 2000, you keep changing that persona willy-nilly. That, in turn, will limit your overall influence as a MediaMaster, causing you to be acceptable – but forgettable.

No matter what you think of Donald Trump, remember that, as he faced the first 2016 state primaries, he was running against 16 other Republican candidates. It was one of the biggest fields ever put forward by the party, but Trump easily dominated from the start simply because he was *not like anyone else*. More importantly, he was very comfortable *being himself.*

While everyone else tried to toe the traditional candidate line, mouthing the standard political platitudes, Trump didn't tamp down his usual brash way of talking. Instead he doubled down on it. Expected frontrunners fell by the wayside, because they seemed colorless and ineffectual next to Trump. You may argue over who was the most qualified candidate – but you can't argue over who was the most memorable candidate. His success was the ultimate triumph of the MediaMaster.

So how do you craft your own Persona of Impact? How do you tap into the special qualities that make you unique – and then leverage them to increase your MediaMaster magnetism?

Let's explore...

CELEBRITY BRANDING® YOU

Celebrity Branding You® was the title of our first Best-Selling book. Its ideas helped lay the groundwork for our Celebrity Branding® Agency by articulating the importance of establishing a personality-driven personal brand. We've been able to successfully help our clients do just that over the years; in the process, we've continued to learn more and more secrets about making that personal brand as powerful as possible.

It all begins with really understanding what a brand is all about. As defined in Wikipedia, a brand is *"a set of marketing and communication methods that help to distinguish a company from competitors and create a lasting impression in the minds of customers."* In other words – a brand is a way to differentiate one product from another, all things being equal.

And when all things became equal is when companies originated the whole concept of brands in the first place. By the 1950s, manufacturing technology had evolved to a point where most companies were offering products of similar quality. That was when the necessity of creating a "brand" became apparent, because those companies needed a way to set themselves apart from the competition. Here's how the evolution was described in an article from *The Atlantic*, "How Brands Were Born: A Brief History of Modern Marketing":

A brand manager would be responsible for giving a product

an identity that distinguished it from nearly indistinguishable competitors. This required an understanding of the target consumer and what we call a "branded proposition" that offered not only functional but also emotional value. Over time, the emotional value would create a buffer against functional parity. As long as the brand was perceived to offer superior value to its competitors, the company offering the brand could charge a little more for its products.[1]

Swap out "product" with "professional," "entrepreneur," "business owner" or "CEO" and the above paragraph still holds true.

Let's say you're a personal injury lawyer – obviously, there's a ton of others in that very same field. Why should people choose you over the rest? Easy answer – if you've established yourself as THE personal injury lawyer in your area. When the public sees your name on a daily basis in commercials, when they see you regularly pop up in online and offline media as a recognized personal injury expert, when they come into your lobby and see a rack of books that you've written on the law, they immediately associate you with being a top-tier professional. That results in them ascribing much more value to retaining you, rather than some other attorney. You've created a prestigious (and lucrative) personal brand – a brand that is based on *what persona you project in the marketplace.*

That projection must be purposeful. In other words, you must have a set of goals in place and methods of achieving those goals when it comes to cementing your Persona of Impact in the public mind.

A Relatable Persona

As you're building your Persona of Impact, you should understand that the way we think about brands in the 21st Century has radically changed.

1 Marc de Swaan Arons, "How Brands Were Born: A Brief History of Modern Marketing," The Atlantic, October 3, 2011

In the past, brands were an object or a hard-and-fast idea to be experienced from afar. You didn't think about having any kind of interaction with a Coke or a Pepsi, you just thought about buying the beverage and drinking it. But now, a brand is more about a relationship. As Sergio Zyman, author of *The End of Marketing as We Know It*, says: *"A brand is essentially a container for a customer's complete experience with the product or company."* [2]

There are several reasons for that. First of all, social media has empowered direct communication with companies and professionals, allowing easy access to a back-and-forth that never existed before. Second of all, innovative new companies like Uber, Lyft and Airbnb have created a whole new business model that's built more on a one-to-one experience. Starbucks also tends to operate as much as a community hub as a coffee shop and even airlines such as Jet Blue and Virgin America operate with more of a relationship vibe.

This trend is summed up by these remarks by Kira Wampler, CMO of Lyft: "Our original tagline was 'Your Friend with a Car' which served not only to describe the human, peer-to-peer experience we delivered with Lyft, but also to differentiate us from other private driver approaches." [3]

That's why it's more important than ever to craft your Persona of Impact as one that's both relatable to people and communication-friendly. The most successful personal brands are ones that reach and touch people on an emotional level, to the extent that the consumer believes they actually "know" that person. It takes some effort to pull off, but it's most definitely worth the effort – and the end result will be greater loyalty, engagement and differentiation.

---

2 Mark Bonchek & Cara France, "Build Your Brand as a Relationship," Harvard Business Review, May 9, 2016
3 Bonchek & France

The Optics of Oprah

Loyalty, engagement and differentiation. Those three attributes definitely apply to the personal brand of Oprah Winfrey, creator of one of the most powerful Personas of Impact in recent history and a top-tier MediaMaster who grew her success to the point where she now owns her own channel - a pretty substantial accomplishment for someone who grew up in poverty as a victim of abuse.

That success comes in part from her strong commitment to being herself. Oprah maintains an incredibly consistent persona – and she is aware of the amount of control she has over this persona. As she has said in the past, "I don't know what the future holds, but I know who holds it."[4]

It's a lot easier to maintain a consistent persona if that persona comes from a place of authenticity, something we recommend to all our clients. As Anna Wintour, the world-famous editor of *Vogue*, said of Oprah, "If you are out to build a brand, you have to know what is real and right for you. The choices that she has made stand the test of time because they are very personal choices."[5]

Your persona too, has to be a very personal choice. How could it be anything but? When you put on different personas like you're trying on a new jacket, you're setting yourself up to look as awkward and uncomfortable as Al Gore did when he walked over to George W. Bush on the debate stage and glared at him.

Instead, your persona has to be an integral part of your real personality. It has to tap into your best and most memorable qualities in the best and most memorable ways. Yes, you may have to work at projecting certain of your qualities and minimizing

4 John Baldoni, "Oprah Winfrey and Your Leadership Brand," Harvard Business Review, November 25, 2009

5 David Carr, "A Triumph of Avoiding the Traps," The New York Times, November 22, 2009

others that are irrelevant or don't add anything to the equation, but that's far different than, say, pretending to be a tough hombre from Waco, Texas when, in reality, you're a sensitive bookworm from Austin.

Just as important to the integrity of your persona is your actual behavior. People are used to "posers" – people who don't back up their words with actions. That's something you never caught Oprah doing – and something people shouldn't catch you doing, especially if you're asking them to trust you with their business.

HOW TO CREATE YOUR PERSONA OF IMPACT

So far, we've given a lot of general information about creating a Persona of Impact – but now let's get down to some nuts and bolts of how to actually make it happen. Generally, a Persona of Impact develops over time through a process of trial and error. But to help you jumpstart your development, we're going to share a five-step process created by leadership experts Norm Smallwood and Dave Ulrich[6] (and modified by us for the purposes of this chapter) that will help you build a strong, authentic, focused and engaging personal brand that will add incredible value to your persona.

Action Step #1: Work backwards from your goals

What do you want to achieve with your Persona of Impact in the next few years?

Do you want to become well-known? If you're already well-known, do you want to attract a certain kind of client or customer that you haven't been able to convert in the past? Do you just want to be seen as more of an influencer in your field? The answer will guide you in creating your Persona of Impact personal brand.

---

6 Norm Smallwood, "Define Your Personal Leadership Brand in Five Steps," Harvard Business Review, March 29, 2010

For example, if you are just looking for name recognition, you may want to do something clever to get your name in front of the public. Dr. Jonathan Zizmor was just one of hundreds of dermatologists in the New York City area when he began his practice. However, once he began putting his name on ads all over subway cars throughout New York City, he eventually became one of the hundred most recognizable New Yorkers.[7] Even though he did this mass transit campaign for thirty years, he said there was a big jump in his business the very first week after he started it.

Of course, if your big goal is to become a thought leader in your profession, then you would be aiming more to produce strongly-branded content, such as a book or series of videos, that demonstrates your expertise, and then find ways to get that content in front of the eyes of potential clients.

Whatever your current big objective, write it down now and continue with the next four steps in this process.

Action Step #2: Determine which qualities you want to be known for.

It can be frustrating when certain positive qualities you or your business possess, somehow get lost in the shuffle in terms of the public's perception of you. Perhaps you're a dentist who's invested a lot of time and money into upscale cosmetic dentistry, but is still mostly known as a professional that merely cleans teeth and fills cavities. Or maybe you're an entrepreneur who's recently earned an MBA in business, but who is still routinely dismissed as an intellectual lightweight.

This step allows you to take another crack at making your overlooked advantages an integral part of your Persona of Impact.

---

7 Billy Parker, "Dr. Jonathan Zizmor, The Subway Doctor," The Gothamist, May 8, 2009 http://gothamist.com/2009/05/08/dr_z.php

First, come up with three descriptors of the main positive qualities that people already ascribe to you – and then come up with three positives you'd *like* to see emphasized in your personal brand.

For example, let's say people already perceive these important qualities in your brand:

- Trustworthy
- Hard-working
- Friendly

But maybe you also want them to see these three attributes:

- Authority
- Innovative
- Professional

Think hard about your two lists of three and write them down – then move on to the next step.

Action Step #3: Define Your Persona

The next step is to combine these six words into three two-word phrases that reflect your desired persona. You'll end up with three new powerful concepts that can help define your Persona of Impact. By linking qualities you're already known for to qualities you want to be known for, you're creating a foundation of credibility to improve your personal brand.

For example, perhaps you might put together the two three-word lists we offered in Action Step #2 to create the following three combinations:

- The Independent Authority (i.e., you know a lot, but you're not compromised by corporate partnerships)
- The Hard-Working Innovator (i.e., you're creative and out-of-the-box, but not flaky or unreliable)
- The Friendly Professional (i.e., you get the job done, but you're also very relatable)

In each case, you're teaming up a known quality with an unknown quality – which validates the unknown.

Action Step #4: Create your Statement of Persona

In this step, you want to take the qualities you put together in Step #3 with the objective you named in Step #1 – then fill in the blanks of the following statement:

"I want to be known for being _____so that I can _____."

For example, let's say in Step #1, your objective was to be a thought leader in your specific field. In that case, your Statement of Persona might read:

"I want to be known for being an independent authority, a hard-working innovator and a friendly professional in order that I can be seen as the leading expert in financial consulting in my community."

After you craft your statement, ask yourself the following three questions to see if you need to refine it:

- *Is this the personal brand that best represents who I am and what I can do?*
- *Does this personal brand create value in the eyes of my customers/clients and the community at large?*
- *Can I follow through on living up to this persona? Am I risking personal credibility?*

You may need to go through some back and forth to craft the best possible Statement of Persona, until it really resonates and you feel totally comfortable with it going forward.

Action Step #5: Road Test Your Statement of Persona

When you're happy with your Statement of Persona, it's time to see if others are as satisfied with it as you are. What you mainly want to look for, as you share the Statement with trusted friends and colleagues, is if it indeed accurately reflects who you are and what you want to accomplish.

It's no secret that many personal brands fail simply because they don't deliver what they promise. Can you live up to your own Statement? Are the words you use to describe yourself and your business accurate? This is the time to find out – before the public figures it out for you.

This process actually might uncover some stronger (and more obvious) qualities that you don't see in yourself; friends can often see us much better than we can ourselves. So don't skip this step, it's important to give yourself a reality check before launching any kind of Persona of Impact.

Of course, your personal brand will continue to evolve over time – so take yourself through this process at regular intervals, say, every other year or so. A Persona of Impact is not static; it grows and changes as you and your business grow and change. Make sure it keeps up with you as you continue on your journey to success.

About Nick

An Emmy Award-Winning Director and Producer, Nick Nanton, Esq., produces media and branded content for top thought leaders and media personalities around the world.

Recognized as a leading expert on branding and storytelling, Nick has authored more than two dozen Best-Selling books (including *The Wall Street Journal* Best-Seller, *StorySelling*™) and produced and directed more than 50 documentaries, earning 15 Emmy Awards and 26 nominations. Nick speaks to audiences internationally on the topics of branding, entertainment, media, business and storytelling at major universities and events.

As the CEO of DNA Media, Nick oversees a portfolio of companies including: The Dicks + Nanton Agency (an international agency with more than 3,000 clients in 63 countries), Dicks + Nanton Productions, Ambitious.com and DNA Films. Nick is an award-winning director, producer and songwriter who has worked on everything from large scale events to television shows with the likes of Steve Forbes, Ivanka Trump, Sir Richard Branson, Larry King, Jack Nicklaus, Rudy Ruettiger (inspiration for the Hollywood Blockbuster, *RUDY*), Brian Tracy, Jack Canfield (*The Secret*, creator of the *Chicken Soup for the Soul*® Series), and many more.

Nick has been seen in *USA Today, The Wall Street Journal, Newsweek, BusinessWeek, Inc. Magazine, The New York Times, Entrepreneur*® *Magazine, Forbes* and *Fast Company,* and has appeared on ABC, NBC, CBS, and FOX television affiliates across the country, as well as on CNN, FOX News, CNBC, and MSNBC coast-to-coast.

Nick is a member of the Florida Bar, a member of The National Academy of Television Arts & Sciences (Home to the EMMYs), co-founder of The National Academy of Best-Selling Authors®, and serves on the Innovation Board of the XPRIZE Foundation, a non-profit organization dedicated to bringing about "radical breakthroughs for the benefit of humanity" through incentivized competition and best known for its Ansari XPRIZE—which incentivized the first private space flight and was the catalyst for Richard Branson's Virgin Galactic. He was a recipient of the Global Shield Humanitarian Award in Feb. 2019.

Nick also enjoys serving as an Elder at Orangewood Church, working with Young Life, Entrepreneurs International and rooting for the Florida Gators with his wife Kristina and their three children, Brock, Bowen and Addison.

Learn more at:
- www.NickNanton.com
- www.CelebrityBrandingAgency.com
- www.DNAmedia.com

About JW

JW Dicks, Esq., is the CEO of DN Agency, an Inc. 5000 Multimedia Company that represents over 3,000 clients in 63 countries.

He is a *Wall Street Journal* Best-Selling Author® who has authored or co-authored over 47 books, a 7-time Emmy® Award-winning Executive Producer and a Broadway Show Producer.

JW is an Ansari XPRIZE Innovation Board member, Chairman of the Board of the National Retirement Council™, Chairman of the Board of the National Academy of Best-Selling Authors®, Board Member of the National Association of Experts, Writers and Speakers®, and a Board Member of the International Academy of Film Makers®.

He has been quoted on business and financial topics in national media such as *USA Today, The Wall Street Journal, Newsweek, Forbes, CNBC.com*, and *Fortune Magazine Small Business*.

JW has co-authored books with legends like Jack Canfield, Brian Tracy, Tom Hopkins, Dr. Nido Qubein, Steve Forbes, Richard Branson, Michael Gerber, Dr. Ivan Misner, and Dan Kennedy.

JW has appeared and interviewed on business television shows airing on ABC, NBC, CBS, and FOX affiliates around the country and co-produces and syndicates a line of franchised business television shows such as *Success Today, Wall Street Today, Hollywood Live*, and *Profiles of Success*.

JW and his wife of 47 years, Linda, have two daughters, and four granddaughters. He is a sixth-generation Floridian and splits his time between his home in Orlando and his beach house on Florida's west coast.

CHAPTER 13

WE REDUCE TAXES BY 50% ALMOST 100% OF THE TIME

BY DAVID GOLLNER & SHERRI MARINI

Business owners, retirees, and pre-retirees, you've done a great thing. You've been 'socking away' money for retirement in a 401(k) or IRA. You've been lowering your tax burden today just like "they" advise you to in just about every publication you have read, deferring tax payments until a later date. By the time you retire at 70, you will have saved the recommended, yet arbitrary, $1 million or more accumulated in retirement savings.

Great! Right? ...Maybe not.

While most people know that they will eventually pay taxes on their IRAs and qualified accounts – those accounts funded by pretax dollars – those same people often fail to consider how much that deferred tax burden will be. They don't understand the tax impact on the money they are squirreling away.

Taxes directly affect your lifestyle in retirement. The more money you hand to Uncle Sam in taxes, the less money you have in your pocket to pay for vacations, that cottage at the lake, or your grandchildren's education. Regardless how you planned to use your retirement nest egg or how diligently you've kept your eye on the prize, paying unnecessary taxes will rob you of those possibilities and more.

WHO IS AFFECTED?

Baby boomers are particularly vulnerable. Now in retirement, many boomers believe that even if they don't need the money they saved for retirement, they can pass it on to their children and grandchildren.

Until the end of 2019, their heirs had the option of spreading out the distributions over their life expectancy and spreading the tax burden across those years. But there is a problem. Tax laws have changed and if you are not working with an elite tax reduction specialist, your retirement might end up looking substantially different than the one you envision.

Don't think you're in the clear if you aren't already in retirement and taking your required distribution. In this case, being younger isn't an advantage. Especially if you are younger with a large retirement investment, ultimately your tax burden will be much greater. Whether you are a 45-year-old with $1 million or a 75-year-old with $1 million, your retirement will be affected by taxes. Obviously, the faster you create a legal tax avoidance plan, the sooner you will start saving.

There are tens of thousands, and in many cases, hundreds of thousands of dollars on the line. If a person has some very large qualified accounts, those taxes could approach millions of dollars.

WHY IT'S IMPORTANT TO ACT TODAY

As of this writing, the federal government owes a debt of over

$23 trillion (see usdebtclock.org). They need to find a way to pay down that debt. Where will they get the money? Conveniently, there is somewhere in the neighborhood of $29 trillion in qualified accounts out there. Imagine the government looking at those accounts like a buzzard eyes carrion. The government is not going to get every penny of it obviously, but if they got a fourth of it back via taxes, that would make a pretty hefty reduction in the debt. Recently, the government moved much closer to that reality. So, baby boomers essentially will be paying for our government's excesses with their retirement accounts.

With the passing of the SECURE Act in December 2019, SECURE stands for Setting Every Community Up for Retirement Enhancements, multi-generational stretch out distributions are eliminated for non-spouse beneficiaries. Previously, you could count on the multi-generation stretch to pass unused retirement investments to non-spouse beneficiaries and allow them to receive that money in installments that kept the tax man away. Under the SECURE Act, however, a non-spouse beneficiary has only 10 years to receive payments from those inherited, qualified accounts, effectively unraveling the tax strategy the investors initially devised and resulting in a substantial increase in the tax burden to their heirs for those years.

The SECURE Act will move the required minimum distribution age from 70 ½ to 72. Which you might assume is better, thinking, "Oh, I can keep contributing now to an IRA all the way through retirement, as long as I have earned wages. That's great!" The truth is the government made this change because they know they're going to get far more tax money from you in the end than they will lose by allowing you to contribute more pretax.

By contributing to qualified accounts, you have entered a contract with the government. Even after the ink has dried on that contract, the government has the option to change the terms of the contract without your input.

Adding to the mounting retirement pressure are the changes established with the Tax Cut and Jobs Act of 2017. These changes last through December 31, 2025, which means the sun is setting on the window to make changes to your retirement plan that will maximize your tax savings in retirement. Many people will want to take advantage of the lower tax rates – possibly utilizing Roth IRA conversions and some sophisticated tax planning to be able to avoid paying unnecessary taxes in the future. In short, if you structured your retirement goals under previous tax laws, you could be leaving money on the table, or worse, flushing it away if you don't adapt your strategy to the new playing field.

WOULD YOU RATHER PAY TAX ON THE SEED OR ON THE HARVEST?

The answer to that question lies in a retirement road map, and the road map looks different for every individual. Many people will tell you it's better to pay the tax on harvest, to wait and see what the yield is. Most people have been taught asset allocation by retirement planners. However, few people look at tax diversification. How much an investor has in tax-free, tax-deferred and after-tax accounts makes a difference in retirement. This is why tax planning is so important. Tax planning looks for tax-reducing strategies that are legal under IRS code that you can benefit from in the current year and for future years. This type of planning is critical in order to have the standard of living in retirement that is desired.

At our office, we begin by completing a nine-page questionnaire that helps us understand everything about our client financially. We use this data to create a retirement road map to demonstrate where they want to go and how they want to live in retirement and what potential pitfalls and roadblocks will keep them from getting there. Then, we create strategies to stretch retirement dollars, so the client doesn't live until 90 years old but runs out of money at 79 years old. We accomplish this by spending a significant amount of time seeking ways to generate tax-free income for them. As fiduciary advisors, our primary concern is the client's best interest. We help them harvest their retirement investments in such a way that even if their yield is more abundant than they anticipated, they won't lose those gains to a ticking tax bomb.

Every investor should assess the road they are on with an experienced professional knowledgeable in tax planning and compare their current scenario with proposed alternatives that might include a variety of financial products. As it turns out, most retirees will have paid back all their original tax savings within the first two to ten years in retirement. How does that happen? Yes, some people are in a lower tax bracket in retirement than they were when they were saving, but when they retire, they historically don't have the tax deductions that they did when they were younger either. Plus, now they pay tax on their social security. Even if they are in a slightly lower tax bracket, they're still going to end up paying more in taxes over the long run.

Ironically, a significant number of retirees will find themselves in the same tax bracket or even a slightly higher bracket than they were in during their working years, due to the loss of deductions, such as the mortgage deduction (as the home is usually paid for in retirement), dependents grown and on their own, elimination of IRA and 401(k) deductions (as they are no longer contributing), taxation of Social Security benefits, and the mandatory distributions from their IRAs and qualified accounts.

So, to the original question, would you rather pay tax on the seed or the harvest? After advising them, most of our clients say, "Well, the seed, of course!" The tax on the seed is known; the tax on the harvest is unknown and can easily be changed by the government at any time without any agreement by the taxpayer.

Every tax dollar saved is a dollar you or your beneficiary can spend on something else. By reducing your taxes by 50% or more, you're preserving the assets you worked so hard to acquire, as well as preserving the lifestyle you planned to have in retirement.

Pre-tax investments are like fast food; it's hot, you get it quick and you get some change back. You feel good in the moment. But it shouldn't be all that you eat. It isn't good for you long term. Eventually, without the right health advice, you pay a price.

DR. JOHN SMITH, A CASE STUDY

Let's look at a case study of a typical physician client of ours whom we will call Dr. John Smith. Dr. John Smith is 71 years old and has a net worth of $2.2 million. About $1 million is in non-qualified accounts including a checking account and a non-qualified mutual fund. The other $1.2 million is in qualified accounts. Dr. Smith has already paid tax on the non-qualified accounts. His only future tax owed on that money will be on any gains to those investments, such as interest, dividends, or capital gains.

Next year, he will need to start withdrawing from that $1.2 million in qualified accounts, but there's a lien on it from Uncle Sam called taxes. Here's the rub. Without proper tax planning for retirement, an investor like Dr. Smith will pay back whatever tax savings they received while they were working in the first few years of retirement.

Dr. Smith needed about $11,000 in retirement income monthly. After social security benefits for his wife and himself, he only needed about a $6,600 disbursement from his retirement accounts each month. Dr. Smith figured he'd live until about age 90. His effective tax rate or average tax rate today was 14.4%. When asked what he thought the tax rate is going to be in the future he estimated 20%.

After taking his required distributions for his life expectancy, we determined he'd be passing on just under $1.2 million. Without adjustments to his current plan, he'd be passing on nearly the same amount of money as he had invested to date (assuming a 6.5% rate of return). The tax bill that would have been due from that would have been at least $238,428, assuming a 20% tax rate.

We showed Dr. Smith several different strategies for tax diversification to deal with the large tax bill that realistically his children would be paying. What's more, it is likely that his children would pay an even higher tax rate because they'd be inheriting the money from him during their peak earning years. Dr. Smith was able to choose an option that preserved the maximum amount of the wealth he had worked so hard to amass utilizing tax advantaged accounts.

First, we were able to show him a way to cover the entire tax bill upon his death for a small percentage of the value of the qualified account. Secondly, we showed him how he could convert $500,000 of the account to 2.1 million of tax-free income for his children upon his death. If Dr. and Mrs. Smith decided at a future point in time to leave less to their children, they would have had approximately one million dollars additional in tax-free income to spend. All of this was in addition to the planning that provided for he and his wife's income needs in retirement on a guaranteed basis, including increases for cost of living adjustments.

The important thing for Dr. Smith, and for you too, is to work with an advisor who understands the intricacies of tax laws and how tax diversification can preserve a retirement nest egg. We reduce taxes by 50 percent nearly 100 percent of the time by employing these strategies. Can your current financial advisors do that?

About David

David Gollner has been helping clients accumulate, manage, protect and enjoy wealth since 1970, when he began his career in estate and retirement planning. David is the founder and CEO of Legacy Financial Strategies, Inc.

David frequently shares his expertise by teaching seminars on IRA's, money management, and estate and retirement planning. His main objective is to establish relationships built on trust and to bring security and peace of mind to his client. Since each client is unique, his recommendations are tailored to each specific client. Regardless of the size of his or her estate, his mission is to show his clients how to increase their net worth, increase cash flow, and preserve their estate.

David Gollner is a graduate of Youngstown State University. He stays on the cutting edge of the financial service industry through continuing education. He is proud to have earned the designation of Master Certified Estate Planner™ and be a graduate of the IRA Institute. David is a member of the International Association of Registered Financial Consultants, the National Association of Christian Financial Consultants and an associate member of the American Bar Association. He also belongs to the Shenango Valley Chamber of Commerce and Better Business Bureau.

David and his wife, Susan, are lifelong residents of Mercer County and reside in Hermitage, PA. They are blessed with three beautiful daughters who, along with their spouses and their six grandchildren also reside in Mercer County. In addition, David is very proud that Sherri Marini, his oldest daughter, joined him in his practice and also specializes in estate and retirement planning. For relaxation, David enjoys attending educational seminars in his field. David feels he is truly blessed as he finds his work to be both relaxing and rewarding.

About Sherri

Sherri Marini is a graduate of Slippery Rock University and received a master's degree from the University of Pittsburgh. She has extensive experience working with retirees. Her experience includes working as Director of Social Services for a 105-bed long term care facility where she served as a resident rights advocate and admissions director, and for the Mercer County Area Agency on Aging as Care Manager for the Family Caregiver Support Program. This program provides reimbursement for respite, supplies, assistive devices and home modifications necessary for the care of elderly family members at home.

In addition, Sherri Marini has worked for three federal government agencies. These include the U.S. Census Bureau as Project Manager, for the National Nursing Home Survey, and for the National Home Health and Hospice Care Survey. In this capacity she received a special award for her original work for the bureau. Sherri also worked for the Office of Personnel Management in the National Security Arena and the Social Security Administration in the retirement, survivors and disability programs.

While Sherri was very successful in her career with the government, she often became frustrated with the bureaucracy and the inefficient manner with which it functioned. Sherri often wondered if what she was doing made a difference. In the year 2000, she made a decision to leave her career with the government and return to Mercer County to join her father's practice at Legacy Financial Strategies, Inc. Sherri specializes in estate and retirement planning. Her diverse knowledge of government programs and real life experience gives her a passion for helping retirees.

As a Registered Investment Advisor Representative and Certified Estate Planner™, she works on behalf of her client's best interests as their trusted advisor. Sherri takes this responsibility very seriously and finds it truly rewarding. Her mission is to help her clients prepare for retirement and ensure maximum choices as clients age and experience changes in their health – protecting them against losing their life savings and helping them maintain a quality of life throughout their retirement years.

Sherri resides in Hermitage, Pennsylvania along with her husband, Michael and her son, Anthony.

CHAPTER 14

IS THERE AN ULTIMATE SECRET TO SUCCESS?

BY JOHN CALUB

All our lives, we have been searching for the ultimate secret to success. Is there really a secret to success? As a global success coach and thought leader, I am often asked by many people this question...

"If you can put together in just one word all the years of the research you've made as to what makes people super successful in every area of their lives, what would be that one word?"

So what will your answer be if you encountered the same question?

My answer to that question is – WISDOM. There are many definitions of wisdom. Most books define it as the ability to think and act using knowledge, experience, understanding, common sense and insight. Wisdom is often associated with qualities such as unbiased judgment, compassion, experiential self-knowledge, self-transcendence and non-attachment, and virtues such as ethics and benevolence. The simplest definition of wisdom that I have ever encountered is: "KNOWLEDGE IN ACTION."

People often confuse the word knowledge as synonymous with wisdom, whereas wisdom is really the key to ultimate success because just knowing a lot of stuff in your head does not automatically give you power. It is when you apply what you know in real-life situations that results in positive outcomes that give one power. So taking your body into action is what drives success.

What comprises wisdom and how does one develop it?

Wisdom is divided into two parts:

- Skillset
- Mindset

Years ago many success gurus taught that skills, the ability to doing something well, is the major factor of success. However, extensive research has recently proven that mindset is more important than skills. In fact, it has been proven time and again now that mindset contributes to 95% of one's success and skills contribute a mere 5%. Now that you know, let's breakdown mindset into specific components so that you can develop your wisdom to a greater extent and reach your full success potential.

Mindset has three components:

1. Mental acuity
2. Emotional acuity
3. Spiritual acuity

   1. The first step in greatly enhancing wisdom is the development of your mental acuity, which is basically the enhancement and continuous improvement of your brain power and cognitive abilities. The first step is including in your diet superfoods, which speed up your thinking process such as ginkgo biloba, dark chocolate, kale, avocado, acai berry, goji berry, bacopa monnieri, etc. And recently, there are now brain development-focused supplements called "nootropics",

which was popularized by the movie, *Limitless*. You can purchase them in popular online shops now. Secondly, your mental factor is greatly enhanced by proper water intake and good sleeping habits.

2. On the other hand, we also need to work on our emotional quotient. This is mastery of your emotions. Many people often flare up or easily get bogged down by simple negative circumstances such as heavy traffic, losing personal belongings, arguments with other people, etc. For this, I highly advise you to look into meditation practices which help you to quickly calm the mind. Emotion is energy in motion. When you cannot easily let go of negative feelings such as hatred, anger, resentment, jealousy, bitterness, fear, envy, etc., our bodies get stuck at not moving into action. One of the two best techniques that I have come across to help you instantly release negative emotions is called EFT, which stands for Emotional Freedom Techniques.

EFT is a simple tapping technique, whereby you touch certain points of the body called meridians, and in doing so, release stuck feelings and negative energy and lets them flow again in just minutes. Another favorite of mine is called the Sedona Method, a questioning technique that, after asking three specific questions over and over again, gets you instantly to a space of complete inner peace.

Again, our moment to moment vibrations, which stem from our feelings, attract to us the same. So. if we are vibrating at low frequency (that means whenever we are sad, angered, revengeful), expect that more and more negative situations will show up in your life. But wherever we can manage our emotions to a point we are always in high vibration (feeling happy, joyful, thankful, inspired, etc.), and we attract positive things into our lives such as good people, good circumstances, more money and more blessings!

3. As regards spirituality, this is basically your alignment with source energy. To succeed at the highest levels, you have to find ways to clear spiritual blockages and the bad karma you have. When we carry past hurts, past dramas and negative childhood programming, they again hold you back from taking action on your goals. To clear spiritual blockages, I recommend a technique called Ho'oponopono, a Hawaiian practice of reconciliation and forgiveness. Each moment you feel stuck and you want to clear things, just say the four phrases:

1) I'm sorry
2) Please forgive me
3) Thank you
4) I love you

and direct it to the Divinity within you.

This clearing is so simple, yet so effective, you can use this moment by moment to get you back to the space where you are clear of past memories, past judgements and past interpretations. In so doing, you begin to clear out problems as solutions, inspired ideas and opportunities for positive change start to manifest in your life. As for karma clearing, one of the easiest methods is to actually do random acts of kindness to offset your karma. Offering to tutor a friend's child without a fee, helping an old woman cross the street and giving a surprise party to someone are just some ways you can erase negative karma.

Lastly, how do you develop your skillset? Although skills contribute a mere 5% to success, skillset is still a factor. The two best ways to enhance your skills is to read books and attend personal development workshops. Find time to read a good book related to your field of choice at least 15 minutes every day. As the saying goes, "Leaders are readers." Secondly, don't be afraid to invest in personal development workshops. Find the best gurus in the field of your choosing and learn from them. Copying is the fastest way to success.

Remember, if you want to be the best, learn from the best. So find your role models and take their wisdom with you. Most people don't go to training workshops because of the huge fees involved. Don't look at them as fees but instead treat them as an investment in yourself. Why? Because every bit of improvement in your skills that takes place will give you a lifetime of return and not just in a single year. I once invested in attending a USD $10,000 10-day sales and persuasion mastery workshop. A lot of my friends and colleagues laughed at me and said it is a big waste of money. However, immediately after that workshop, and using the methods I picked up in that training, my sales grossed over eight figures in that same year!

With the above, I hope I was able to give you three very important pillars, on which you can lean your ladder of success and be assured of authentic happiness and freedom. You now have a simplified framework on what you need to work on that will bring forth the ultimate secret of success to you, and take you to the field of your highest dreams and aspirations – WISDOM. As what we realized from the life story of the richest man who ever lived, King Solomon:

... seek wisdom first and success in all areas of your life will follow.

About John

John Calub grew up in extreme poverty in his early childhood years after his parent's house, which was situated in a remote province in the Philippines, got burned. After this awful situation, his parents migrated to the city of Manila hoping to find a way to get back up financially. However, years passed and their economic status barely improved. This was about the time that John started dreaming of transforming his life to help his parents get out of poverty.

John learned selling at a young age and was able to send himself to University of the Philippines by selling household products to his classmates during breaks. From there, he graduated with two degrees, namely a Bachelor of Science in Economics and a Bachelor of Science in Business Administration.

After graduation, he worked as an entry-level executive for several years until he found himself becoming a part-time writer for the biggest newspaper company in the Philippines. His assignment was to interview successful people as to how they reached the top and kept themselves there. This led to John's turning point, where he got a chance to meet Jack Canfield, who at that time was doing an international book signing for his best-seller entitled *The Success Principles*. John interviewed Jack and was invited to attend his one-day seminar on success.

After applying the principles he learned from Jack's book and his live seminar, John went on to become a sought-after sales consultant to top corporations in his country, and immediately rose from being broke to becoming a multi-millionaire in less than one year.

Today, John Calub is recognized by the biggest media companies in his country as the Philippines' number one success coach and persuasion guru. He is the founder of John Calub Training International, an academy for personal development. His workshops have already produced thousands of success stories and multi-millionaires in Asia. He is the founder of Success Community, the fastest growing online-mastermind group in the world, with membership growing at an exponential rate. He has been quoted in publications like *Forbes Magazine, Entrepreneur*, et al. His amazing life story has been featured in two *New York Times* best-selling books of Jack Canfield namely, *The Success Principles* (10th Anniversary Edition) and *Living The Success Principles*. He has been personally mentored by top global business gurus the likes of John Maxwell, Robert Kiyosaki, Tony Robbins, Brian Tracy and billionaires Donald Trump and Richard Branson. His book *Abundance Factor*, which he co-authored with Dr. Joe Vitale, made it to number one best-selling book in Amazon in one category. Lastly, he co-hosted *Success Secrets*, a nationwide TV show viewed by millions.

On the lighter side, John is now happily married and blessed with two kids. He loves travelling the globe with his family every year. In his spare time, he collects gold toys from all over the world, and dreams of making his toy collection part of the *Guinness Book of World Records*.

You can connect with John at:
- www.facebook.com/johncalubtraining
- https://www.linkedin.com/in/johncalub/

CHAPTER 15

TRAINING FOR ENTREPRENEURIAL SUCCESS

BY KUMAR MANU ("MANU")

It was 1973, when Bill Gates got admitted to Harvard College, a legendarily "very difficult" and highly-coveted school. Getting the acceptance letter must have been a truly hard pursuit, and must have been a matter of immense pride and joy for Bill and his loved ones. Yet, he dropped out in just two years to follow his dream of seeing, "a computer on every desk in every home" through Microsoft, a company that made Bill a millionaire by the age of 26 and is today one of the most recognizable brands on the planet. These days, as Microsoft continues being a leading innovator, Bill himself devotes much of his time to philanthropy and giving back large portions of his wealth to the world at large, through the Bill & Melinda Gates Foundation.

What is success for Bill? Has it always been the same? Was it ever about the money?

And what success do you seek? And what disciplines can you train yourself in to get to it?

Read on…

Discipline #1: *Be Purposeful, Passionate, Proud*

The critical first discipline for YOUR success is YOUR thorough understanding of what success would look like for you. Be your own person … *get inspired but don't imitate anybody else!*

Introspect, consider that success may not be all the wealth you have, or the people you command. It is a feeling, a state of mind. It's about accomplishing something that excites you, gives you joy, makes you proud. As Bob Dylan said, "What's money? A man is a success if he gets up in the morning and goes to bed at night, and in between does what he wants to do."

As you read these lines, you are obviously on the journey of personal betterment for success. Ask yourself, *what's your purpose?* How do you feel when you think about it? How much do you enjoy the moments you spend on the purpose? Who are you serving, and what difference are you making to them through your efforts?

One technique to help discover or solidify your purpose is *"Vision"*. Close your eyes and imagine… visualize yourself in the state of success as you've defined for yourself. Does it make you feel good? Is it really something you want to do? Save this image somewhere in your brain so you can see it over and over. The more vivid this image is, the more effective it will be. It'll always guide you, inspire you, give you the all-important "Why?" to help you make decisions and deal with challenges you'll inevitably face on your road to success.

With purpose goes belief. More than believing in what you want to succeed in, develop belief in your ability to achieve that success. *Watch for and stay away from self-doubt.* Albert Bandura, an influential social cognitive psychologist, concluded several decades ago from a series of experiments, that perhaps the best predictor of individuals' success is whether or not they believe that they'll succeed. *Don't get held back by your current reality* – say, your current skillset – instead, apply your passion to *push yourself and make time for gaining the new mastery needed* for what you want to achieve.

<u>Discipline #2:</u> *Be Results-Focused, Action-Oriented, Accountable*

Vision without Action is hallucination. Countless people the world over go to bed with ideas and aspirations that get lost in the day-to-day, right after alarm clocks ring the next morning. But the only place where success comes before work is the dictionary. So, it's important to take action... *Start!*

Borrowing an example from soccer, to score a goal you must play, right? And playing doesn't mean just standing there, or even running around randomly. It requires keeping an eye on the ball, passing or receiving it at the right time, and running with it when needed, against all hurdles. For this, you must *choose your attitude* – one that holds you accountable for your success. The more you feel accountable, the harder you'll play – automatically. Similarly in life, *start by starting.* When it comes to following your passion for success, don't wait for the right time that'll never arrive.

Then take steps to prevent your dream from becoming one that never transforms to reality… make regular progress – even daily – capturing small wins along the way that will add up towards the ultimate success you desire. *Consistency and cadence* are imperative. You can't lose weight by planning to exercise non-stop for a month at the end of the year. However, by exercising 30 minutes a day, 4 times a week, you certainly will! Regularity amounts to practice, causing what is known as *"Automatization"* – that refers to practicing a skill to such an extent that it becomes virtually routine. Think about the first time you rode a bike. It was difficult, you needed training wheels, and somebody to help you. It was all you could focus on at the time. But after years of doing that, now you don't even think about it as "something you need to do." It just happens! Think… what actions can you "automatize" to increase your productivity and reduce stress?

And make sure you *keep score* of your wins. Knowing how far you've come and how far you've left to go on your journey will help you decide if you need to course-correct, develop new strategies, seek help, or even pivot. Regularly measuring progress is another way for you to keep you motivated and improving, but make sure you don't overdo it, spending more time looking at the map trying to get somewhere, and not focusing enough on your driving and enjoying the view.

Finally, keep a *to-do list* of ideas crossing your mind to support your quest, review these ideas regularly so you can line them up to act on them in a timely manner. But be wary about starting on too many of them at the same time. Manage your time, prioritize. When you find yourself overwhelmed with too much work, then _stop starting and start finishing_. It is important to "keep accomplishing" – it'll boost your confidence and make you wiser.

Discipline #3: *Be Open-Minded, Curious, Flexible*

While "just doing it" is the best way for you to find for yourself what it would take for you to bring your Vision to life, also be open to external insights supporting your thought-process. For example, this book. Such learning is critical to validating your thoughts, enhancing them, providing new ideas, and even giving you strength and confidence for your pursuit.

Bill Gates, having started as a self-taught computer expert, these days reads about one book every week on a variety of impactful topics (several not even close to the world of computers, by the way), which he now graciously shares on his personal blog at gatesnotes.com.

It's reasonable to say that not everybody would have the luxury of time to read as much as Bill Gates, but when it comes to avenues to learn and get inspired, work with what you can, at the pace you can afford, including blogs, articles, videos, and podcasts. Attending an immersive learning session (typically 2-4 days) is an investment you will find worthwhile in the big scheme of things. Also, several successful individuals I know draw upon personal coaches and mentors for continuous improvement.

And remember, *thou shalt be flexible!* You must be open to integrating new learnings into everything related to your success, right from your definition of success to what you do day-to-day to achieve it. In fact, about the former, while you must commit yourself passionately to a goal, at the same time consider it a hypothesis that you should be constantly testing through your actions. This approach will significantly keep you on track for success in a changing world, and your own changing self. In fact, you should *fail fast and often* (reflecting each time), rather than fail once and catastrophically.

Also, *ask a lot of questions...* to yourself or to your mentors. How could you do something better? What else could you be doing? Are you missing something? And so on... don't be shy in asking questions. Remember – "He who asks a question is a fool for a minute, he who doesn't is one forever." (Ancient Proverb).

All these are your options to keep getting stronger and better to face the challenges lurking on your way to success. And challenges there will be... for which let's go over Discipline #4.

Discipline #4: Be Optimistic, Perseverant, Resilient

There's no such thing as an overnight success. When you hear of one, you're simply witnessing the moment when the world got wind of the success. But the long, hard journey that precedes that moment is like a large, heavy flywheel that was slow and hard to turn at first, but gained momentum on every push to ultimately get to the moment when the world saw it turning effortlessly.

Just like the egg, which one day suddenly cracks open with a beautiful chicken emerging out of it, with no indication of the preceding slow, long (and quiet, by the way) growth it underwent within the confines of the shell.

So, *give yourself time to succeed*; of course, as long as you're consistently persevering for your success during that time.

Now imagine you plan to drive from New York to San Francisco. Despite your confidence in your driving ability, and even if you have the best car in the world to drive, you can still fully expect delays and detours along the way. Maybe you already account for those in your travel time estimates. But if you don't apply the same principle to your own life, why won't you? Shouldn't it be obvious that you should expect the unexpected?

Unfortunately, in many cases, it isn't. Many people start with rosy dreams of "the happy path" – which expose them to disappointment and anxiety. Don't be one of them... *expect failures, setbacks and ambiguity!* An ancient proverb says, "One who cannot tolerate small misfortunes can never accomplish great things." So, when a setback arrives, how you respond to it will define you. Absolutely *don't lose heart*, welcome it with optimism, because "this too, shall pass", So *face it, accept it, deal with it, and move on*, because you believe in your purpose and in yourself, and are doing what it takes.

Discipline #5: Be Friendly, Kind, Genuine

It is true that, "It takes a village..." No person is an island, and your success will depend on the feedback, help, good wishes and blessings from the *support system* of those you come in contact with through your travails.

Be social (and not just the "social-media" kind, but in-person), welcome conversations, and *make time generously to help others.* You'll learn from others, and earn joy from helping them … it will energize you, enhance you, and boost your self-confidence about making a difference. Remember, success is not just about you achieving your goals, but also how you do, feel and improve along the way.

<u>*Discipline #6:*</u> *Be Balanced, Energetic, Motivated*

Don't be all work and no play... enjoying the journey is as important as the destination. Engage in activities, develop regular habits that will raise your energy, well-being and overall "feel-goodness" – all important ingredients to *supercharge YOU* for success. Some options I would offer are exercise, eating well, practicing abstinence from stimulants like alcohol, watching funny videos, reading books, group activities (golf, tennis, poker, yoga... anything counts), cooking, mindfulness, and getting enough sleep!

The road to success is uncertain and long, bound to have unexpected turns, and requires extreme perseverance. You being supercharged is essential to your success... Isn't it?

BRINGING IT ALL TOGETHER

You will be a successful entrepreneur. You have the desire, and there are certainly things out there that you will be successful at. The following six disciplines of success are your playbook for a <u>*strong, well-rounded and supercharged YOU*</u> as the foundation.

1. Be Purposeful, Passionate, Proud
2. Be Results-Focused, Action-Oriented, Accountable
3. Be Open-Minded, Curious, Flexible
4. Be Optimistic, Perseverant, Resilient
5. Be Friendly, Kind, Genuine
6. Be Balanced, Energetic, Motivated

Good luck, and I hope to keep hearing about your continued journey of successes!

About Manu

Kumar Manu ("Manu") is a Coach and Author with a passion for empowering individuals, organizations and himself with proficiency in fundamental strategies and tactics for transformation and improvement.

As Founder and CEO of Summit Next Global, Manu brings expert-led, high-impact, immersive learning experiences in competencies critical to success in an ever-changing world. Over the years, Manu has internationally helped individuals and teams from all walks of life conquer hurdles and achieve success by harnessing their innate potential and gaining new skills.

His service, spanning the spectrum across personal, team, leadership and organizational development, strategy, transformation, and results-maximization, is the synthesis of this experience, established practices, research, and his "forever a student" mindset.

CHAPTER 16

SUCCESS FOUNDATIONS: BUILD THE FLOOR BEFORE YOU BUILD THE WALLS

BY JENNIFER ANDERSON

As I scrolled through my email inbox to prioritize my responses, my eyes stopped on a message titled "Please Call Me ASAP" from Tom, a former client. I learned during a series of calls over the next couple of days that Tom's landlord, Eric, had been found unresponsive in Tom's home and that Eric had a business, several homes and bank accounts all requiring urgent attention. He had opened a small business that became quite successful, and he began to invest in real estate with some of his profits.

Unfortunately, Eric had not registered a business entity. He had not done any real planning in any area of his life, nor had he consulted any professionals or mentors. He had not established any legal, insurance, financial, or tax foundations. He had not signed important agreements for business and personal decisions other than the bare minimum required by third parties, like his franchisor. He had not investigated the best way to run his type of business, or to address the flurry of liens and penalties for unpaid sales taxes and property taxes, and other employee and government challenges that followed. He succeeded his way to bankruptcy – implosion by accidental success without a strong foundation.

Facing these challenges without a foundation of personal and business solutions and liability protection sent Eric on a downward spiral that intensified each year. I began to create a plan to untangle the tangled web of problems for his estate and closing the business – the business that could have survived his death – if he had incorporated and had established a business succession plan to manage the payroll and client fulfillment needs. Many business owners are so busy working in their business that they fail to work on their business growth. They ignore the opportunities for their business to become their legacy after they stop working. They become a slave to their business, which can become an expensive hobby or a low-paying, life-depleting job if not properly managed or planned.

What would happen to Eric's pending clients? Will his employees be paid? Could his business possibly continue at all? Without Eric available, is it possible for someone to coordinate the desperately needed roof repairs for his rental property? We struggled to piece together the pieces of his legal, insurance, financial, tax, and personal life with no roadmap - with no Eric or anyone else with knowledge of where to find anything other than public records in each category. We frantically searched his office and intensely investigated whether Eric had an attorney or any other resources for his business and personal decisions.

As I began listing all the tasks necessary to fix Tom and Eric's predicament, my mind flashed back to the other business challenges I witnessed – attorneys whose new practices failed because of inadequate planning for business taxes and employee management; companies who spent hundreds of thousands of dollars on lawsuits to correct breaches of contracts cobbled from online templates without advice; landlords left without recourse because their management practices and do-it-yourself (DIY) leases did not protect them from the tens of thousands of dollars in damage their judgment-proof tenants caused to their property.

In all areas of life, when we set goals and begin to act to achieve those goals, the path to achievement can be so much easier and sustainable if we build a strong foundation to support our growth. We must take intentional, planned action, and model our success using a support system and the best resources to create our own growth framework. This list can help anyone who has a goal avoid the implosion by success plight so many of my clients experience, so we can achieve success more smoothly and comfortably and build a lasting legacy.

1. <u>Remember the Rule of LIFT:</u> Have a solid Legal, Insurance, Financial, and Tax plan (if you have property or want to have property). Find qualified professionals in these categories. If you are starting a new business and do not have much interaction with other owners, contractors and employees, and customers/clients, do it yourself ("DIY") is okay during the early stages. Do not try to use DIY tools for these categories as you accumulate more property, or as your business grows, unless you are trained in each area. Attorneys without insurance, financial, tax and marketing/ sales training struggle opening new businesses. Accountants without legal training can struggle making proper employee or contractor management decisions if they don't also have legal training. Some skills in business growth should not be outsourced until you prove you can weather challenges in that area consistently.

2. <u>Obsessively Maintain Your Inner Work:</u> Sometimes we all fall into the trap of thinking we don't have time for anything except the list of never-ending activities that pop into our head as our "should do" list. Many of my clients insist they don't have time for any activities that nurture their souls, that connect them with their inner strength and values. However, sustainable, smart growth requires doing the inner work first

before the outer work. Natural ebbs and flows will occur in all aspects of life, and we can weather all challenges better when we maintain our connection with our inner strength and values.

Before each day, each meeting, any event that might challenge you or require a lot of your energy, meditate or revisit your source of strength. Living life in calm control of your emotions and mind will help activate the genius of your prefrontal cortex versus the "fight or flight" reflexive responses. Exercise your emotional control "muscles" so your inner genius controls your decisions and actions. Practice meditation. Listen to brain entrainment audios, affirmations, and guided visualizations. Use self-hypnosis to help open communication between your conscious and unconscious minds; build your skills in positive self-talk.

Intensely connect the emotions you want to feel with your written goals and vision board every morning. Exercise and play. Fear and anxiety decrease blood flow to the frontal lobe, which is the part of the brain responsible for logical planning and optimal decision-making. Take planned, controlled and inspired action toward your goals after you trigger positive mental states that stimulate your inner genius in the prefrontal cortex.

Connecting with your inner strength every morning and before each segment of your day will help you maintain motivation and mastery of your mental state so you can follow your plan more effectively. Keep a list of the most effective tools for you, the tools that quickly connect you with your strength and value, so the best version of you can show up in each segment of your day.

3. Calibrating Plans On Failures: There is no failure, only feedback. That said, preparing for "failure" and forming a strong awareness of the consequences of that "failure" are

both crucial elements of bouncing back from a setback. After "failure," we can wallow in the negativity – the shame, guilt, sadness or fear – or we can learn the lessons from the feedback, calibrate our strategies and processes, and tweak our plans. There are times we all receive negative feedback in our personal or professional lives. In fact, if we are not getting negative feedback, we are probably not trying hard enough to grow. After "failure," we can choose to wallow in the negativity, or we can learn the lesson and adapt. Having a strong mindset and strong personal and business foundations make it so much easier to bounce back from "failure," and "failure" can offer powerful lessons that are more deeply etched in our memory banks about the best habits in our personal and professional lives.

4. <u>Written Goals and Plans Reduced Into Manageable Pieces:</u> Write your goals for career, relationships, family, personal growth and development, health and fitness, and any other category that you value for balance in your life. Write your goal in detail for the next year, quarter, month, etc. Begin with your annual goal for each category and imagine it as a vivid, detailed image that can become a jig saw puzzle with pieces that can fit into smaller blocks of time. Reverse engineer your success by breaking the bigger goals into smaller goals. What quarterly goal is necessary to achieve the annual goal? What monthly goal is necessary to achieve the quarterly goal? Each week, list in detail all the tasks that will be necessary to reach the monthly goal and determine what professionals or other people and resources are required to complete the tasks. Identify the ONE most important task that you SHOULD do to move you toward the weekly, monthly, quarterly, and eventually the annual goal. Listing in detail all the necessary tasks for each chunk of time helps you delegate more effectively so you can master your schedule and follow your plan.

5. <u>Find Mentors and Models:</u> Model your growth and build your plans with guidance from people who are where you want to be in the longer-term. Discover their strategies, what professionals advised them, how they set up their business and their life for success – and follow a similar or the same path. Mentors and models can make the learning curve much more manageable, so you can understand what size foundation you need at each stage of growth. Learn from the mistakes your mentors and models made, not by making your own mistakes. We don't know what we don't know and maintaining connections with mentors and models of success can help us avoid obstacles we wouldn't see coming. They also help us see when we are stuck in a rut or are not using the most effective strategies in our life and career.

6. <u>Segment Intending:</u> So many people interpret one challenge in a day as a signal that the whole day must be "bad." Labeling a day, week, month, or year based on a couple of experiences robs us of our opportunities to restart ourselves and our businesses at every moment. Begin each day setting an intention for the day overall and an intention for each segment of the day based on how you want to feel and what you want to accomplish during each segment. Note what must happen during each segment of the day for you to feel the intended feeling and achieve the desired result. Calibrate your feelings and your accomplishments frequently during the day, at a minimum once during each segment, so you can course correct and remind yourself whether you are on track with your plan.

7. <u>Obsessive Honesty And Compassion For Yourself:</u> So many of my clients are afraid to admit to me or to themselves the challenges and mental states that hold them back from success. During each moment of reflection and calibration, be aware of your emotions and track your progress. Be honest about what emotions and challenges might hold you back. Use mentors or like-minded friends as accountability partners.

Find help when you're stuck. Everybody experiences highs and lows and you can find a solution to every problem if you are honest with yourself about what problems exist, and seek help accurately identifying the problems or roadblocks as you follow your plan. Be kind to yourself and understand that everyone faces challenges. Once you accurately identify the problem, ask someone who has overcome the same problem or experienced your challenge and ask for help. Everyone experiences challenges, negative emotions, and limiting beliefs. Identify those disempowering states with compassion for yourself. Diagnose the problem states so you can treat them and progress more effectively along your growth plan.

8. <u>Implement:</u> Seek advice from trained or experienced people, and follow their advice. I once asked a client how well a particular motivation technique I taught worked for her, and she replied that it worked well when she remembered to use the technique. We all have resources available to help through challenges, but our action plans and support resources only work if we actually implement them. Create the habit of reviewing your list of resources and automatically searching for the best tool for each challenge. What are the small hinges that open big doors? Remember to search for those hinges and use them so you can progress more rapidly and follow your plan more diligently.

About Jennifer

Jennifer Anderson, Esq. helps her clients grow their businesses by creating strong personal and business foundations and growth plans to transform businesses into legacies. She is an attorney licensed in Texas and is certified in neurolinguistic programming, hypnosis, and Timeline Therapy. Both as a student and as a consultant, Jennifer has trained in enhancing performance and productivity in all areas of life for more than 20 years. She has dedicated her career to helping clients solve problems, overcome limitations, and achieve success in their personal and professional lives.

After graduating from University of Texas – Austin and the University of Houston Law Center, Jennifer dedicated her legal practice to assisting entrepreneurs with their business, real estate, estate planning, and elder law needs. Jennifer's passion lies in helping clients avoid legal costs through educating and empowering clients to improve their quality of life and their income. Jennifer's business consulting focuses on training business owners in building strong infrastructures and enhancing growth through achieving peak performance states. Jennifer also guides her clients to create a strong legal foundation, and advises regarding legal claims and opportunities to resolve conflicts without expensive litigation.

As a mother of three, she understands the importance of providing convenient, efficient services that promote quality of life and business success for clients facing the challenge of balancing career and family schedules. When not working with entrepreneurs to build their business legacy and preserve it for future generations, Jennifer loves spending time with her husband and three children, watching Longhorns and Spurs games, studying personal development courses, and any and all beach activities.

To contact Jennifer:
- Email: janderson@andersonlawtexas.com
- Websites: andersonlawtexas.com; jenandersonconsulting.com
- Facebook: Anderson Law PLLC; Jennifer Anderson Coaching and Consulting

CHAPTER 17

THE PILLARS OF FAITH, COMMUNITY & HUMOR

BY VIVEK CHANDRA

My story that I share with you is one of immigrating to the United States from Barh, India. I grew up with my family in India, where my father enrolled my brother and I in what he thought was a temple, but was actually a Christian school. My father said it didn't matter to him as they all led to one master. I had a wonderful childhood, and my family and I would spend time with another family and travel to a sandy section of the river Ganges for New Year's Day and cook food and celebrate. During the holidays we would go to the village and participate in the community dramatic theatre.

I started learning English in the 10th grade. I was one of the top students in my grade which helped me receive a national level scholarship, which, along with my knowledge of English, helped pay for my education and the fee to study at an engineering college. In 1986, I was accepted into a good University – all credit due to a brilliant professor in my hometown. His grasp of Newton's laws were amazing and the University was later renamed The Indian Institute of Technology – Roorkee. I had an incredible support system within my family, and my father taught me that no one should ever feel inferior if you had less materialistic things. My mother created a support system that would eventually help me create a new life in the United States.

I was then married to my wife through an arranged marriage my father set up – and I didn't get to meet her until our wedding day. My wife and I then moved to Los Angeles with only six-hundred dollars; we had no credit and I struggled to obtain my driver's license – which I received after several attempts. My wife and I then decided to move to Colorado where I was able to get a job and put down roots. We were excited to see snow there for the first time in our lives. My first son was born in Colorado. I was working and we had a stable income and comfortable living.

Then 9/11 happened and I was ultimately laid off from work when the economy took a turn for the worst. When I found a job in San Francisco, I had to commute between Colorado and California every week. It became difficult to maintain a work and home life, and my wife was becoming unhappy with the situation. My wife ultimately earned her Master's degree in Information Technology and Management, and became the prime earning member of the house. She was instrumental in building a strong understanding of mathematics and studies in our home with the children. Moving to the United States and starting over with my family was difficult, but with my foundation strong in my faith, community and humor, we prevailed as a part of the American dream.

I was re-introduced to my faith when I met a man in San Francisco who turned out to be my cousin. He gave me a lot of advice about faith and we would meet up during our free time and talk about our faith. He told me to leave everything to God and just do my best. My vision of God changed after a meeting with my cousin and his friends when they explained that God has a kinetic and static energy. Since then, I have been trying to seek truth. During my mornings, I chant *"karagre vasate lakshmi, kar madhye saraswati, kar mule tu govinda, prabahte kar darshanam."* That is to remember the goddess of wealth (Lakshmi), the goddess of knowledge (Saraswati), and Lord Vishnu as he is one of the three bigger deities (Shiva, Brahma, and Vishnu). I was also introduced to the concept of guru which has been changing all over the world.

There are two types of guru's. The first guru's intentions are to either take your money and commit crime, or perform self-service. The second type of guru's intentions is to remove poverty, create positivity, and perform "yagna" so that all people have access to food. For me, faith comes from different directions. My faith is not limited to Gita, or the King James Bible, but it helps me stay grounded and guides me in moments of crises and for wisdom, peace and prosperity. I have often taken refuge in 16th century Indian poetry. I found their philosophy very practical, and I found Rahim and Kabir to be some of the greatest poets of India.

I was raised, with guidance from my Father, with a deep connection to our community and giving service back to it. It is the moment in time and space where we live and have our roots. I began volunteering at local foundations at a young age helping young people of color. Giving back gave me a feeling of being connected to my community. One experience I had with helping in my community was when a student was getting down off a bus and was hit by a truck. He ended up losing one of his legs. I helped raise $236,000 for his surgeries (including a donation from my wife).

In our community, you could get involved in various programs, from sports to housing to mentorship. I later connected with a professor who was an editor of a local English daily magazine. I spent a considerable amount of time writing articles there as well as at the radio station. Giving back to your community, no matter how small, plants seeds to be nourished for years to come. Even mentoring someone else can leave an imprint that you were not expecting.

I also believe humor is important because my father had a good sense of humor and helped me with techniques to make myself feel better when I was down. Laughter and humor helped me to deal with situations that were difficult and also when I was hurt. Studies have shown how humor has been a positive factor in dealing with mental health with many long term and short term benefits. Just watching a sitcom or even a cartoon has shown improvement in stress relief, relief of pain, and mood enhancement in us. I love to watch reality shows, old movies, and listen to old music from Bollywood or Hollywood. I believe comedy should have a starring role in life – it's my way of dealing with situations when I get hurt. A good sense of humor also helps people in times of grief.

These three core principles, Faith, Community and Humor, have helped me transition as an immigrant from India to the United States with $600 in my pocket and a new wife. I encourage everyone to implement any and all of these principles.

1. Faith

Find time in the morning to pray. Prayers for wisdom, grace, peace, and a moment of gratefulness. Whether you pray to God, Buddha, or some other deity, having faith provides a greater inner strength to persevere through times of stress and can help you discover a deeper purpose in life. Faith also gives hope to you when you need it most.

2. Community

Volunteering and becoming committed to your community provides an enormous amount of benefit – particularly if you are new to an area. The social benefits of engaging creates lifelong bonds with your community, and imparts a sense of responsibility to those around you. You are also helping to provide a better quality of life to the public and paying forward a positive effect for those who may need it the most.

If you don't know where to start, look at a local women's or men's shelter, your local church, or even an organization like Habitat for Humanity. Volunteering can also improve your career prospects as well.

3. Humor

Studies have long shown that laughter can be the best medicine for the soul. Laughter has long shown it is a good way to release tension, and improve mood. There are even studies that have shown that it can help protect your heart and have benefits for cardiovascular problems. In 2006, a Norwegian study found that people with a sense of humor have a 30% better chance of survival when dealing with a severe disease. It has shown to improve mental and emotional health which is a major component in the cause of disease.

Whenever you feel sad or disconnected, try to find a way to laugh. Your body may not know why you're laughing, but the benefits will still be there. I've learned I've had to find a way to laugh through my tribulations of moving to the U.S.A., and I couldn't be happier.

About Vivek

Vivek Chandra is a Senior Database Administrator. He has been helping companies in the Information and Technology field for twenty years. Despite having a degree in Civil Engineering, Information and Technology is where he has excelled for most of his career.

Before moving to the United States in 1995, Vivek attended Patna University in Patna (the eleventh oldest university in India). Patna University attracted many famous Convocation Speakers over the years, including Lord Mountbatten, the last Viceroy of India, and the acclaimed scientist C.V. Raman.* At Patna, he was able to improve his Sanskrit and English, as well as improve his skills in debating.

This education later gave him the ability to author many publications. Despite all of the social upheaval in India at that time, he used his knowledge and three years of critical work experience to make the difficult decision to move from his home country of India to the USA.

Vivek also was part of an Environmental Planning Course that took place in Rishikesh and Haridwar. There, he was able to study and observe the speed of growth in the Ganges in Rishikesh. To be able to attend the course in these two holy cities with the wisdom of his peers was a great honor. Although he was challenged by his instructors at the beginning, he was congratulated both by them and his peers when it was completed.

In his middle school years, Vivek and a friend of his used to publish a newspaper and try to sell it to business owners. Now, Vivek is trying to reconnect with his teachers in the small city of Barh. Although Vivek has written many articles about Information Technology and the Architecture of India, he is trying to reach out to his old connections to join hands and write more articles that will be based on both global and domestic events.

Vivek has a keen interest and focus on Conflict Resolution, because finding a commonality among all of us is the key to peace. These are principles he has lived by, and ones that helped him flourish in America.

* https://timesofindia.indiatimes.com/city/patna/a-university-with-a-glorious-past-but-a-perilous-present/articleshow/60341668.cms

CHAPTER 18

THE GIFT OF GRATITUDE

BY GWEN MEDVED

At times, our own light goes out and is rekindled by a spark from another person. Each of us has cause to think with deep gratitude of those who have lighted the flame within us.

~ Albert Schweitzer

An amazing thing happened as I was writing this chapter. I had spent weeks trying to find the one perfect story that would exemplify all the ways that gratitude has contributed to my success and happiness.

Unable to decide what to write, I set my alarm to go to bed, said a prayer and asked for guidance on how to best share my message. Within a few minutes, I received a text! I expected it to be from one of my daughters, most likely my oldest, Claire. She had been sending me encouraging texts all day about how I needed to just write like the way I talk. The message, however, was from Jan Moberly, my first grade teacher; she was someone I had not seen in decades, although we are Facebook friends.

It read:

> *"My friend, and your old second grade teacher, Mrs. Bauer,*

lives close and we were talking last night. She has a teenager living with her to finish the year. The girl thanked her for doing it and Mrs. Bauer told her that someday she would have the opportunity to help someone. I mentioned that you had reminded me of staying with us one summer, so I told her what an amazing woman you have become and about your beautiful daughters. She wanted me to say hi, and that she is proud of the woman you have become."

I immediately started crying as I read through these beautiful, unexpected words. This message was coming from an earth-angel woman who changed my life over thirty years ago, and to whom I am forever grateful. She felt compelled to write to me at the exact moment I had asked for guidance. There are no coincidences in life, and so, with a heart full of gratitude, I said a prayer of thanks and knew this was the story to tell.

You see, as a teenager, my family life and home was so dysfunctional that the only choice I had to survive was to leave. With nowhere to go, my grade school teacher invited me in. Freshly divorced and feeling a bit lost herself, we made a perfect match. She gave me unconditional love and acceptance at a time that I needed it most. She taught me how to see the light through the darkness, and most importantly, she believed in me and showed me how to believe in myself. More than anything, she gave me something to be grateful for.

Jan was gentle, patient and very kind. I think she recognized something in me as well. Being freshly wounded herself, I think she understood that too much goodness of anything would tip me over the edge or maybe push me away. It would take me a while to trust what she was offering. She took it slow and let me take my time in warming up to her. She never acted offended or put off when I was short, or uncommunicative. She gave me exactly what I needed in order to heal from the wounds of rejection and being displaced from my home.

Most of all, Jan never treated me as a pity project. She treated me as a person, and by doing so, she allowed me to keep my self-respect when I felt unworthy, discarded and unloved by my family. I will never be able to give back to her the gift that she gave me at that time. She was an absolute salvation. I have spent my life with an attitude of gratitude and a desire to pay forward the love and random acts of kindness I have received at just the right times throughout my entire life. Jan is a good woman who showed me there are good people in the world. She let me know that I was one of them and that I was worthy of being treated well. Her kindness allowed me to be grateful for someone and to believe and trust in the world again.

Gratitude is the most loving and precious gift we can give to ourselves. Gratitude can heal past traumas, and help us navigate our way through difficult circumstances and life challenges. Gratitude allows us to acknowledge what is positive in each situation so that we can use it for personal growth. *Recognizing who and what you have to be grateful for, especially in the worst times of your life fosters resilience, and resilience is the key to success.* If you can take each hurdle or obstacle in your life, and find something good in it, or learn a lesson from it, then you are further ahead, not behind. This is the art of achievement. Learning your lessons and taking them with you as you march forward.

Gratitude leads to resiliency, the superpower that allows us to bounce back when bad things happen and get back up when we are knocked down. This is why gratitude is the foundation of all success. We must get back up and try again each time we are knocked down.

After Jan took me in, I got back up, with her help, and felt energized with a new budding confidence. I began to set goals believing I could achieve them. I made plans for the future with optimism and excitement knowing I could create a good life for myself. I felt confident I could navigate adversities in life. Each adverse experience became an opportunity to affirm my ability to overcome life's difficult moments. Every obstacle became something to be grateful for later, because of the valuable lessons it brought me.

Graduating from high school, I was alone, without my parents or any family there to congratulate me. Then there was: Sexual misconduct by a trusted adult; working full time for a year before going to college *while living independently and taking a full-time course load at the local university*; accumulating $70K in student loan debt; becoming a wife and a mother before either my spouse or I had an income; investing precious savings early on in products that failed, and failed, then failed again; balancing insane amounts of relationship stress while growing a young family and a commission-based business at the same time; bringing my father-in-law home to die in our arms after a debilitating stroke when the hospital said it was impossible, AND getting my own father through cancer treatment long distance, AND running a manufacturing business I knew nothing about for two years because my father-in-law passed. *All at the same time I was trying to stay focused on raising my daughters ages 4 and 6, help grow our business from the sidelines, while supporting my husband in his massive grief?* And finally, infidelity that nearly destroyed my marriage, crushed my family, shattered my heart, and broke my trust in the world … again.

These are just a few examples of what life has thrown at me, because that is what life does. It throws out a bunch of challenging situations, loss and heartbreak too. You get to choose how you handle what you are not in control of, not what is thrown at you. Finding what to appreciate and be grateful for even in the worst of times creates an attitude of gratitude that will foster the resilience needed to overcome whatever life may throw at you. My own determination to stay grateful is what got me through every time.

Today, I choose to view my non-traditional, and dysfunctional upbringing with gratitude and use it as a huge advantage and gift to help others. I offer my clients and partners an empowered approach to any circumstance that comes along. Fresh ideas and strategies help my clients create new perspectives and ways to identify, and then achieve their goals. Most importantly, I give them relatable real-life examples of how to use gratitude to shift their mindset and their energy into a place of prosperity and success.

I have learned that success comes one failure at a time if you are willing to gratefully look for what each experience can teach you. Asking these questions, when things don't turn out the way you want them:

- What is it I can learn from this?
- What is this telling me?
- Is there an opportunity for growth here?
- What can I be grateful for?
- What are the gifts hidden inside of this?

The best news is, you can begin to choose gratitude at any time in your life. Although it is a habit, or "practice", below you will find ways in which you can adopt the fabulous "attitude of gratitude" that will change your life. Each of us chooses how we view any situation, or circumstance. Are we looking for the positive, or are we anchored in the negative? Gratitude is a decision to focus on what is right, instead of what is wrong.

Here are some simple gratitude practices in the form of a 21-day challenge. For 21 days, make a commitment to write in a gratitude journal daily and choose at least one of the other exercises listed below. Why 21 days? Science has shown that it takes 21 days to create a new habit. Practicing these exercises rewires your brain into a state of positivity and gratitude.

The 21-day gratitude challenge:

1. <u>Journal every day:</u> Record at least five things, occurrences,

people that you are grateful for. What happened today that you can be grateful for? This is difficult because of everything we take for granted. The clean air we breathe, the car we have to drive, the birds singing outside, our health, and the health of our loved ones.....

2. Meditation: Meditation is incredible for creating peace and positivity. There are many guided meditations online and in Apps. When you practice gratitude meditations, your mind shifts automatically into a place of appreciation and even joy.

3. Gratitude jar: Write something on a piece of paper that you are grateful for and drop it into a jar. Physically witnessing the volume of your gratitude grow is a powerful affirmation.

4. Gratitude reflection: Speak your gratitude out loud with this sentence stem, "today I am grateful for...", and try to go as long as you can. This one always makes me cry because my heart is so full of love for all that is right in my world.

5. Letter of gratitude: The letter of gratitude is one of the most powerful ways to forgive and release pain and hurt caused by past events and trauma. It can be written to yourself or anyone in your past or present.

I have dedicated my life to practicing and teaching the art of gratitude, to foster resiliency and success. I hope you feel inspired to begin living a life of deep gratitude. One that includes self-acceptance, forgiveness, and a deep appreciation for all that is right in your world. Once you begin to intuitively and automatically focus your energy and attention on what is right and well in your world with deep gratitude, you will become a magnet for the success that you desire.

About Gwen

Pregnant, unmarried, and $70,000 in debt, Gwen Medved was a struggling graduate student with a life-altering decision to make—continue living life with a heart full of anger and regret or find a way to forgive herself and those who abused and abandoned her.

Gwen took the high road, and within three years she was a loving mom with her degree and a million dollars in the bank!

A successful entrepreneur, author, speaker, trainer, and coach with a deep commitment to family, Gwen speaks with a "compassion of truth," that makes her relatable and creates an instant connection with her clients and audiences.

Gwen has a unique and inspiring personal story to tell of what it takes to succeed when opportunity is not handed to you. An author of *Pillars of Success* and *Life Lessons of Success*, executive producer of *"It's Happening Right Here,"* a documentary film on human trafficking and the rescue work of Tim Ballard's Operation Underground Railroad, Gwen's greatest belief is that love and real connection are what is desperately needed to transform the anxiety, depression, numbness, disconnect and dissociation that is epidemic in today's world of overwhelming technology and de-humanizing social media influences.

Gwen is dedicated to bringing her experience to entrepreneurs, community leaders, corporate employees, and all women ready to tackle the challenge of letting go of the past in order to succeed in the present. Through live events, retreats, women's summits, speaking engagements, and private coaching, Gwen is here to teach her clients, audiences and small groups how to succeed, rise and thrive through adversity.

Gwen holds a B.A. from Purdue University and an M.Ed. in Counseling and Human Services from DePaul University. She is a certified Canfield Transformational Trainer, Values-Based Leadership Coach and Health Coach, and advocate for women, children and families.

CHAPTER 19

FROM BROKEN TO BOUNDLESS
A YEAR OF BELIEVING IN THE UNBELIEVABLE

BY PAUL BROWN

It's not what happens to you, but how you react to it that matters.
~ Epictetus

I had seen this quote or something very similar to it countless times in my life. It is by the Greek Philosopher, Epictetus, and although I understood the premise, I don't know if I ever truly believed it. After all, we've all had things happen to us at one point in our lives that we just couldn't overcome, right? Little did I know that one day I would put this quote to the test, and my life and that of my kids would lie in the balance.

The Event:
In mid-December of 2018, I was forced to do one of the most challenging things in my life. For the safety of my kids and myself, I had to have my partner, the love of my life, and the mother of my child, removed from our house. After 7 years of struggling alongside her, I was left with no other alternatives. In the end, here are the circumstances that faced my family:

- I became a single dad of two kids, ages 4 and 13.
- We would be involved in a court case and decision about the outcome of my kids.
- Since I had to call the Department of Children & Families (DCF) for assistance, they would be in our lives for the foreseeable future.
- It was ten days until Christmas and 14 days until my daughter's 5th birthday, and our bank accounts had been drained and credit cards had been maxed out.
- I was 56 years old and 25 lbs. overweight.

The Reaction:
Things were undeniably tough, and it took me a couple of days to get over my state of shock, but I knew I needed to move on. At that time and against all evidence, I knew I needed to be positive. I knew I needed to forget the facts that confronted me and simply start believing in something better. I needed to believe in myself. I needed to believe in a better future. And, I needed to believe that I possessed the willpower to never give up.

Once I believed the future would be okay, I set out to create that better future for myself and my kids. I began by imagining my future without limits or boundaries. To envision any and all outcomes that came to mind. In the end, I settled upon a few goals that appeared attainable, yet at that moment were quite a stretch. Next, I needed to create a plan to get to this future. My plan began with the idea that I needed to find more energy to successfully manage my way through the rigors and stress of single-parent life. To accomplish this, I knew my fitness level needed to increase. In short, for me to function in my new role, I had to visit the gym regularly, eat better, and lose 25 lbs. along the way. Although I had always strived to keep my life in balance, I realized that this was more of a time for obsession than it was for moderation. It was time to get to work.

I was certain the future was going to be better, and when I started to take action, I was amazed at how quickly things began to happen. In my first week back at the gym, I received messages that I had won three separate prestigious beverage awards. One of these awards included my image on the cover of Cheers Magazine. I also started to lose weight and even received an unexpected sum of money that helped see us through Christmas and my daughter's birthday. These things happened so much sooner than expected that I was quickly approaching the idyllic future I had just created in my mind. It was already time to go back now and imagine an even better future.

So, at the end of this 12 months, what do our lives look like?

- The kids are happy, healthy, and thriving in school. My daughter graduated from preschool and is now in kindergarten. My son is having a great year in 8th grade and is looking forward to high school.

- Just six months from that life-changing day in December, I was granted full custody of the children. I know there are a lot of horror stories out there about dealing with the Department of Children and Families and our court system and in some cases these may be true. Our experience with both was overwhelmingly positive, however. DCF worked closely with us and provided a wonderful level of support. I am thankful for their friendship and assistance and will make sure the office we worked with receives a copy of this book. The Court experience was positive too, as I never even felt the need to hire an attorney. From what I saw, if you are honest, respectful, follow directions and truly put your kids first, you can have a positive experience as well.

- My career continued to thrive, and we are enjoying some financial stability for the first time in many years. I will be entering my 9th year of employment with the same company and remain thankful for their support throughout this process. I am also leveraging my knowledge and experience with a variety of exciting new products I will be launching this year.

- I lost 25 lbs. and my fitness level hasn't been this good in years. My fitness goals changed dramatically throughout the year and I ended up setting a World Record for Endurance on an Elliptical Trainer. I traveled 73.4 virtual miles on an elliptical in 12 hours. This would have been impossible to even imagine back in December 2018. This summer, I will look to better this record as I attempt to travel 135 miles on an elliptical in 24 hours. I have also become a spokesperson for a men's health clinic and have had numerous interviews about this elliptical event and raised money for charity along the way. Not a bad year for that overweight 56-year-old that thought he might be over the hill.

To create this transformation, I followed a 5-step plan I call BIPAD, which stands for Believe, Imagine, Plan, Activate and Deliver. I can tell you with full confidence that if you follow this simple plan outlined below, you, too can achieve similar results.

1. Believe – Before anything positive is going to happen to you, you first need to believe it will. You don't need the complete vision and details to start this process. In fact, it may be better if you don't have it all worked out, yet. Simply begin to believe in yourself, your success and your future. Believe passionately and purposefully and with no regard for the facts. This important step will set you on your way to success.

2. Imagine – Once you truly believe that your future will be okay, then you need to start creating it. This is the fun part of the process where you get to make your wildest dreams and fantasies come to life in your mind. Find a quiet spot and immerse yourself in this exercise which is almost the opposite of meditation. In meditation, you allow thoughts and visions to pass right through your stream of consciousness. With this exercise, you hold on to those thoughts and visions as they appear and even build upon them. Once you believe anything is possible, your mind will create a future that you truly couldn't have dreamed of before.

3. Plan – With your dreams in mind, you now need the roadmap to the future. This is where you put together a detailed step-by-step process that will lead you to that destination. The more steps you can add to this plan the better. This will help you build momentum later as you begin to finish these steps and mark them as complete. Remember, there may be some detours along the way as things don't always go as planned, but this is okay. Your route may change as long as the destination remains the same.

4. Activate – Look at everything you have accomplished already. Is it time to sit back and wait for the positive results to start coming in? Nope, it is time to get to work. Time to put that plan of yours into action and start on the journey towards your new life. If you are on the right path, you will enjoy the process because this is where you will start seeing positive results. Put in the time and effort here because as you follow your plan, you will begin to move closer to your destination. What are the words that keep me active and moving forward during this phase?

Rise, Grind and Repeat!

5. Deliver – Now you have knocked those first four steps out of the park; however, they don't mean anything if you don't finish the tasks at hand and deliver the goods. I am writing this section the same day Kobe Bryant, his daughter and several others died in a tragic helicopter crash. I didn't know Kobe or his family, but he always inspired me with his work ethic. He had otherworldly talent, but he was also one of the hardest working athletes ever. All that talent and hard work would have been somewhat wasted; however, if he didn't also possess the mindset of a closer. Time and again, Kobe showed that he wanted the ball in his hands when the game was on the line. No moment was too big because he believed in himself and his ability to deliver.

There are other examples of great closers in the sporting world, such as Michael Jordan, Tiger Woods, and Joe Montana, to name a few. But being a clutch performer is not restricted to just sports. In fact, the ability to deliver, close, finish or be defined as a clutch performer is necessary for every pursuit. Don't excel at all other facets of this plan and then fail to follow through because you become scared or uncomfortable when it is time to deliver. Those feelings are natural but will quickly fade away when you push through and see the results you are able to deliver on the other side. Be comfortable with being uncomfortable. And just like athletes, you may not be successful with every attempt, but I promise each time you step up to deliver, it will become a little easier.

So, there's my story — a remarkable 12-month transformation that began with my believing in the unbelievable. When I look back, I hardly recognize the person I was a little over a year ago, but I love him for putting all of this into action. With each step forward, I gained confidence, momentum and a greater belief in the vision I had created for the future. And my transformation is only accelerating. My plans for the next 18 months are enormous and the 5-year vision I now have for myself and my children is so exciting that there is no way I am going to miss out on one single day of this process. And please know that I am neither special nor extraordinary. In fact, I did a great job of proving this fact for 56 years. If I can transform my life, I promise that you can, too.

So now it's your turn to get started towards a better future. Start believing, start imagining, start planning, start taking action and start delivering those results. A year from now, you will love yourself for doing it. And don't worry if there are some failures or missteps along the way. If you're not failing, you're not trying, learning or pushing yourself far enough.

So now that you've read my story, how are you going to react? Can I suggest that you take that leap of faith and start believing in yourself today? Your future self will thank you.

About Paul

Paul Brown is CEO of Paul Brown Productions and National Beverage Manager of Front Burner Brands. As a beverage professional, endurance athlete and dedicated philanthropist, Paul Brown is driven to inspire and support others on their own journeys to success. In his professional life, Brown is known as an award-winning National Beverage Manager for Front Burner Brands and The Melting Pot Restaurants. Within the fitness world, he holds the World Record for endurance on an elliptical trainer and plans to top his best in 2020 by completing 135 miles on an elliptical trainer in just 24 hours.

Paul, with his professional expertise and compelling story, is a co-author of *Pillars of Success*, an inspirational success guidebook due out this year. He is thrilled to be collaborating with Jack Canfield, author of the *Chicken Soup for the Soul* series, to publish his first book.

Paul Brown will be featured in *Entrepreneur Magazine* later this year and credits a never-ending belief in working towards a better future as his biggest asset when it comes to delivering results. As a single father in his late 50s, Brown says he's probably the last person one would expect to be setting endurance records, but his innate drive for success and to help others is strong. And he is further motivated by how challenging himself has worked to rally others to unite and create positive change. Brown's fitness fundraisers have helped to raise funds and awareness for St. Jude's Children's Research Hospital and Americans Against Opioid Addiction. It's an accomplishment Brown is incredibly proud of, and one that fuels him to take on even bigger challenges.

Highlights of Paul Brown's career include serving on both the *Cheers Magazine* and the Millennium Advisory Boards for food and beverage marketing. He has won several awards in the restaurant industry space for his beverage programs, event promotions, special offers and more. Paul Brown is a certified mixologist whose professional experience includes work in chain restaurants, hospitality and brewing companies, and major companies including, Sheraton Sand Key Resorts, Front Burner Brands and Melting Pot Restaurants.

Paul also plans to expand his entrepreneurial beverage projects and continue using his increasing fitness prowess to benefit important causes in the Clearwater, Florida community and beyond.

Contact information for Paul Brown:
- Email: pbrown1178@gmail.com
- Website: www.paulbrownproductions.com
- Instagram: @pbfitat50
- Facebook: https://www.facebook.com/paul.brown.7921

Fun Fact - Paul's Top 10 Recommended Follows on Instagram:

David Goggins @davidgoggins
James Lawrence @ironcowboyjames
Jack Canfield @jackcanfield_official
Jesse Itzler @jesseitzler
Jocko Willink @jockowillink
Joe Rogan @joerogan
Leonardo Dicaprio @leonardodicaprio
Rich Roll @richroll
The Rock @therock
Tom Bilyeu @tombilye

9 781733 417648